Teaching Across Borders

Teaching Across Borders

Empowering English Learners

Nesreen El-Baz

BLOOMSBURY ACADEMIC
NEW YORK · LONDON · OXFORD · NEW DELHI · SYDNEY

BLOOMSBURY ACADEMIC
Bloomsbury Publishing Inc, 1359 Broadway, New York, NY 10018, USA
Bloomsbury Publishing Plc, 50 Bedford Square, London, WC1B 3DP, UK
Bloomsbury Publishing Ireland, 29 Earlsfort Terrace, Dublin 2, D02 AY28, Ireland

BLOOMSBURY, BLOOMSBURY ACADEMIC and the Diana logo are
trademarks of Bloomsbury Publishing Plc

First published in the United States of America 2026

A catalog record for this book is available from the Library of Congress

ISBN:	HB:	979-8-216-37605-7
	PB:	979-8-216-37604-0
	ePDF:	979-8-216-37607-1
	eBook:	979-8-216-37606-4

Typeset by Integra Software Services Pvt. Ltd.
Printed and bound in the United States of America

For product safety related questions contact productsafety@bloomsbury.com.

To find out more about our authors and books visit www.bloomsbury.com
and sign up for our newsletters.

To Layla, my granddaughter
tomorrow's hope that rises with the dawn.
May you reach beyond the clouds
with courage and wisdom,
keep your spirit tender and bright,
and let your voice,
even in silence,
always be heard.

To my sons,
the echo in every classroom where I've stood,
the reason behind every true word I could,
the heartbeat beneath this journey.
You were my first lessons in love
and my greatest teachers in growth.

Contents

Preface ix

Author's Note on the Use of AI Tools xi

Part 1 Heartfelt Beginnings: The Spark of Teaching 1

1 A New Beginning 3

2 Embracing Differences 7

3 Fostering Diversity and Inclusion in the Classroom 13

4 Teaching Experiences Across Two Campuses 21

5 Stepping into the Teacher's Role 25

Part 2 Bridging Cultures and Emotions in the Classroom 31

6 Connecting Hearts and Minds 33

7 Empowering Diversity Through Cultural Sensitivity 37

Part 3 Teaching Strategies for Language Development 43

8 Bringing Vocabulary and Culture to Life Through Images 45

9 Crafting Personal Narratives Through Visual Inspiration 55

10 Taking Personal Narratives to the Next Level 63

11 Descriptive Writing: Connecting Language to Life 77

12 Interactive Listening and Speaking 83

13 Using Picture Books and Read-alouds to Enhance Language Learning 89

14 Creative and Hands-on Approaches to Teach Literature 95

15 Empowering Readers to Pass High-stakes Exams 101

Part 4 Empowering English Learners and Teachers for Success 111

16 Unlocking Potential 113

17 Meeting the Specific Needs of Students 123

Part 5 Advanced Tools for Classroom Innovation 131

18 Cultivating Growth: Building Skills as an Educator 133

19 Using Technology to Develop Language Learning 143

20 Co-teaching 157

21 Data-driven Teaching 167

Part 6 Conclusion and Resources 173

22 Full Circle: My Journey of Growth 175

23 Three Research-based Lesson Plans for Teachers 183

Preface

Education has always been more than just a job for me; it's been a journey of self-discovery, connection, and purpose. I'll always be grateful to my parents. Even though money was tight when I was growing up, they made sure I learned English. They believed it would open doors for me, and they were right. Their sacrifices lit a fire in me, a deep love of learning that I've carried into every classroom and every student I've met since.

And then there's my husband, my quiet champion. He believed in this book even when I doubted it myself. On days when I wasn't sure my voice was worth hearing, he would gently remind me: "Write it for the kids, for the grandkids." That always brought me back to my "why," a real desire to share what I've learned with others who want to make a difference.

There's a quote by Ludwig Wittgenstein that's stayed with me for years: "The limits of my language mean the limits of my world." For me, learning English wasn't just about communicating with more people, it expanded my world. It opened up new cultures, new ideas, and new ways of thinking. It showed me that language isn't just a tool; it's a bridge to opportunity, belonging, and growth.

From a young age, I saw education as the key to reaching for what once felt impossible. My parents' belief in learning gave me the determination to make sure others, especially students who've had difficult beginnings, could access those same chances.

Over the years, I've worked in classrooms around the world, teaching students from all kinds of backgrounds and languages. Those experiences taught me how powerful it is when a teacher creates a space where everyone feels seen, included, and encouraged to grow. I learned to be adaptable, creative, and deeply aware of the emotional landscape every learner carries.

This book is a reflection of those lessons. Inside, you'll find practical, classroom-tested strategies for supporting English learners; not theories, but real tools. I explore how to use visuals to teach storytelling and grammar, how to gamify learning to increase engagement, how to guide students in narrative writing, and how to use virtual field trips to expand their worldview. Each chapter is rooted in experience and focused on equity, belonging, and voice.

If you're a teacher, I hope these pages offer inspiration and tools you can use to build classrooms that feel welcoming, empowering, and joyful. If you're a school leader, I hope this book reminds you how important it is to support teachers and create school cultures that celebrate diversity. And if you're a parent, I hope you'll find helpful ways to stay involved in your child's learning—and be reminded that education doesn't only happen at school.

My journey through different school systems and cultures has shown me just how powerful good teaching can be. The lessons I share in this book come from both personal and professional experience, and I offer them with humility, gratitude, and hope.

To my incredible colleagues, thank you for the ideas, support, and collaboration. You've helped me grow more than you know. To my students, your curiosity, resilience, and energy have been my greatest inspiration. Teaching you has taught me just as much in return. And to the mentors who walked with me, thank you for reminding me that patience, reflection, and one kind word can change everything. I would also like to thank Professor Hosam M. Mahmoud, Department of Statistics, The George Washington University, for his encouragement and support.

Finally, to my husband: thank you for standing quietly behind me while I found the courage to write. Your faith in me gave me the strength to believe my voice mattered. This book exists because you believed in the version of me that didn't yet exist, and that gift is everything,

As you read, I hope you find ideas that inspire action, stories that offer encouragement, and strategies that help you uplift the learners in your life. Together, we can build classrooms and communities where every student, no matter where they come from or how they speak, feels seen, supported, and ready to shine.

Author's Note on the Use of AI Tools

In the preparation of this manuscript, I made limited use of artificial intelligence (AI) tools as part of my creative and editorial process. These tools were used solely to support my writing, such as for brainstorming, refining sentence structure, and organizing ideas, and not to generate substantive content or replace my role as the author.

All material presented in this work is original, and I take full responsibility for its content. Where third-party content (including images, quotations, or references) is included, all necessary permissions have been obtained in accordance with the terms of this publishing agreement.

AI was used ethically and under human oversight. The final text reflects my own voice, intent, and intellectual contribution, consistent with the professional and scholarly standards of authorship.

Part 1
Heartfelt Beginnings: The Spark of Teaching

1   A New Beginning

The year was 2006, just a week before the start of the school year in Houston, Texas. Dark clouds gathered overhead as rain poured steadily, matching the storm brewing inside me. I stood by the window, wondering if I could truly step back into the professional world after fourteen years at home. Teaching was in my blood, a calling I had always felt destined to pursue. From an early age, I had admired my teachers, captivated by the way they sparked curiosity and inspired a love of learning. But now, as the rain beat against the glass, doubt began to creep in. Could I still be the educator I once aspired to be? Returning to the classroom wasn't just about rekindling my career; it was about rediscovering myself beyond the roles of wife and mother. The idea stirred excitement, but it also carried a quiet weight, like standing at the edge of a bridge that led somewhere unfamiliar, not knowing exactly what I'd find on the other side.

As I wrestled with these questions, the rain softened, and sunlight broke through the clouds, casting warm golden rays across the room. It felt like nature itself was offering me reassurance, a sign that clarity often follows the stormiest skies. This small moment of light felt like a lesson I would later share with my students: growth requires discomfort before clarity emerges. Looking back, I realize this moment of personal uncertainty helped me empathize with my students, particularly English learners, who, like me, were stepping into an unfamiliar world. Despite my hesitation, I knew I had to move forward. I was driven by a desire to rekindle my passion for teaching and to step into the light of possibility once again.

My journey as an educator had begun years earlier in Cairo, where I graduated from the Faculty of Linguistics at Ain Shams University. Soon after, I married an engineer, and our family embarked on a life that would take us across continents. In Aberdeen, Scotland, where my children were just three years old, I encountered the British education system for the first time not only as a parent but also as an aspiring educator.

During our time there, I earned my teaching certificate from Trinity College in London, marking my first official step into teaching. Over the years, our journey continued to Japan and then Paris, each location offering its own challenges and opportunities. In Japan, I marveled at the discipline and precision of their educational system, while in Paris, I admired the emphasis on critical thinking and debate. These experiences broadened my perspective and taught me that education is not confined to a single method or system. Instead, it is a fluid, evolving process shaped by the cultural and societal values of each community. By the time we settled in the United States in 2004, I had gained a wealth of knowledge from diverse educational landscapes. However, transitioning into the American system was a new challenge entirely.

Standing at the threshold of this new chapter in Houston, I was determined to bring all I had learned to my teaching journey. With sunlight breaking through the clouds, I felt ready to apply my global perspective to the American classroom. Yet, I also understood that my journey wasn't just about applying what I knew—it was about learning anew. The best teachers, I reminded myself, are lifelong learners. As I prepared for my role as an English for Speakers of Other Languages (ESOL) teaching assistant, supporting students in both Arabic and English, I found strength in the idea of being different. My unique background felt like an asset, yet uncertainty lingered. How would my experience as a non-American fit into this educational landscape? Having chosen British schools for my sons in the past, the American public school system was unfamiliar, not just for them but for me as well. As I watched them navigate new assignments, teaching methods, and expectations, I realized their journey mirrored my own.

Over time, I came to appreciate the American emphasis on fostering independence and critical thinking. This shift in perspective helped me see what my English learners needed to succeed: a balance of independence and support. Like my sons, they were adjusting not only to a new education system but also to the cultural expectations that came with it. One student, Ahmed, stood out to me during those early days.

Ahmed had recently immigrated from Syria and struggled to follow the classroom routines. His teachers were frustrated by his lack of participation, but I saw a boy who was overwhelmed, not unwilling. By slowly guiding him through small tasks, celebrating his successes, and encouraging him to share his experiences in class, I watched him transform. His progress reminded me of the power of patience and the importance of meeting students where they are.

Starting in the American system felt like taking my first steps all over again, not just as a professional, but as a learner. The district offered a six-hour training session for new teaching assistants, and one piece of advice stood out: "Be open to feedback. Let others observe you, and accept their feedback." This simple yet profound lesson reshaped my mindset. Teaching, I came to understand, is a dynamic process that thrives on reflection and refinement. Even the most experienced educators have room to grow. This philosophy became a cornerstone of my teaching approach: to view growth, feedback, and adaptability not as challenges but as opportunities to better serve my students. Shortly after starting my role, I encountered my first cultural misstep: speaking during the Pledge of Allegiance. The embarrassment was immediate, but so was the lesson. Teaching wasn't just about understanding the curriculum—it required cultural competence and awareness of the unspoken rules that shape a school's environment. This experience reminded me that humility and curiosity are essential in navigating new systems, both for me and for my students.

Looking back, these early challenges laid the foundation for my work with diverse students. They taught me to approach teaching with flexibility, humility, and an understanding that cultural differences, when embraced, can enhance the learning experience. Like my students, I had to navigate unfamiliar territory, and this shared experience deepened my empathy and connection with them. My journey taught me that as educators, we are not just transmitters of knowledge—we are guides and learners ourselves. The best teaching happens when we embrace change, value feedback, and see growth as an ongoing process.

I hope my story inspires others to approach education with openness and courage, empowering the next generation to see their own potential and thrive in an ever-changing world.

Teacher Tip

Starting a new teaching job? Yeah, it can totally feel like being tossed into the deep end. But trust me, you're not alone. One of the best things you can do early on is just spend time with other teachers. Watch how they run their classrooms, connect with their students, and deliver lessons. You'll start to notice little things that feel right to you, steal those! Build on them. Remember, you don't have to invent the wheel. Don't be afraid to ask questions, and be open to feedback. Every single day is a chance to get better. Teaching's a journey, and with every step, you'll grow a little more into the kind of teacher you want to be.

Parent Tip

Change is hard, especially for kids. A new school or a different routine can really throw them off. A teacher once told me, "I feel for kids who are new to the culture. It was hard enough for me, so how must it feel for those youngsters?" His words stuck with me. So, how can you help as a parent? Start by keeping the vibe positive. Talk about the fun stuff: new friends, new things to learn, new chances to grow. Show them how to stay organized. Encourage them to speak up when they're unsure, and help them feel okay asking for help.

At the same time, stay close. Check in. Listen when something feels off. Cheer them on. When they know they've got your support, but also the freedom to figure things out, they'll settle in and start to shine.

2 Embracing Differences

As my heart raced against my ribs and my hands trembled, I stepped into the school's spacious library, where clusters of teachers and staff chatted and laughed as if they'd known each other forever. The sound of their conversations filled the room, a stark contrast to the nervous silence in my mind. I felt a swirl of excitement and unease, as if I were stepping onto a stage without knowing my lines. Many smiled at me, and I nervously smiled back, but I couldn't shake the feeling of being an outsider. Even my name, "Nesreen," felt foreign in this space, adding another layer of uncertainty to my first day. I introduced myself as "Nesreen" as it appeared on my passport, though I preferred the original pronunciation, "Nesreen." It was a small adjustment, but one that reflected the complex journey I was about to begin.

It wasn't until later in my teaching career that one of the district English as a Second Language (ESL) coordinators approached me and said, "I heard your voice message, and it's Nesreen with a long 'e,' isn't it?" That moment was profound because it was the first time I felt I had reclaimed my name. In that moment, I realized that reclaiming my name wasn't just about me, but it was about setting an example for my students. By embracing my identity, I could encourage them to embrace theirs. It was a small but powerful way to show them that their stories and their names mattered. This experience made me realize how important it is for students, especially those from diverse cultural backgrounds, to feel seen and respected. Acknowledging and honoring their names became my way of creating an inclusive classroom, a place where they could embrace their identities and feel like they truly belonged.

Many of my American Asian students would use their American names, as listed in the register. But I made it a point to ask them their original names and how they preferred to be addressed. Most students chose their original names, and I made sure to pronounce them correctly. Over time, this simple practice became a celebration of diversity that enriched our learning environment. Students began to share more about their cultures, traditions, and even the meanings behind their names. It wasn't just a gesture; it became a foundation for mutual respect and a sense of belonging. In a classroom setting, trust is essential for fostering a safe learning environment where students feel comfortable taking risks with language and participating in discussions. When students feel respected, they are more likely to engage with the learning process, which leads to stronger academic outcomes. It wasn't just about getting the names right; it was about fostering an environment where their identities were embraced and celebrated.

I remember one Chinese student, Jennifer, who introduced herself by her American name, but when I asked for her real name, she said, "Yingting." I asked if she preferred to be called Yingting, and she nodded. From that moment on, I called her by her chosen name. Years later, in 2025, I contacted her to ask permission to include a letter she had written to me. Though she now goes by Tiffany, she warmly encouraged me to use her original name, Yingting, and expressed how much it meant to be part of my journey. Her response reminded me that small acts of care, like honoring a student's name or preserving their words, can have a lasting impact on a young person's sense of self. This act of asking and honoring each student's choice was not just a gesture of respect; it was also a teaching strategy that helped build trust and rapport.

In one class, after I had asked a few of my Chinese students about their name preferences, Mariana, a curious student from Mexico, raised her hand and asked, "Ms., can you tell me what my Chinese name is?" Her question caught me off guard, but I smiled and explained that Chinese names are unique to Chinese culture.

Moments like these turned into valuable opportunities for cross-cultural learning, allowing students to share their backgrounds and learn from one another. Encouraging students to ask questions about different cultures helped to create a more inclusive and empathetic classroom, where diversity was celebrated as a strength rather than a barrier.

That day, I realized how much I still had to learn in this new chapter of my life. But I wasn't alone in this learning process. A tall blonde teacher, Ms. K, introduced herself as the head of the ESOL department. She welcomed me warmly, and her genuine kindness helped me feel like I belonged. Ms. K's warm welcome didn't end with that introduction. Over the weeks, she became a mentor, sharing insights about the students, the community, and how to bridge cultural gaps effectively. Her guidance reassured me that I was not alone in this journey, and it reminded me of the importance of having a support system as an educator.

Looking back, that first day was more than an introduction to a new school, it was the beginning of a journey that would teach me as much as I would teach my students. In that lively library, I took the first steps toward creating a classroom where every student, regardless of their background, could feel seen, valued, and empowered to learn.

During our first staff meeting, the principal read a letter from a former student who was now in juvenile detention. In the letter, the student expressed deep gratitude for his teacher, saying:

You believed in me when I didn't even believe in myself. You saw something in me that no one else did. I'm here now because of my own mistakes, but I want you to know that I remember everything you taught me, not just about school, but about life. I'm doing my best to get out of here, and I hope to make you proud one day.

As I listened to the words of the letter, I thought about the countless students who might feel unseen or unheard in their daily lives. This letter reminded me that the simplest gestures, a word of encouragement, a moment of patience could plant seeds of hope that might not bloom until years later. It was a humbling reminder of the unseen ripple effects of teaching.

Education is not just about academics, but rather about reaching into a student's heart, inspiring hope, and nurturing potential. This story reinforced the critical role relationships play in teaching. Building strong relationships with students helps them feel valued and understood, which in turn motivates them to engage more actively in their learning. As teachers, we are not just imparting knowledge, we are helping shape their identities and futures by showing them we believe in their potential. This sentiment stayed with me and shaped my approach to teaching, reminding me that sometimes, what students need most is for someone to believe in them.

Following the principal's heartfelt speech, we headed to lunch. Ms. K continued to share insights about the school and its students, especially the challenges many of them faced outside of school. Her commitment to supporting every child, regardless of their background, was inspiring. Working alongside colleagues like Ms. K and Ms. G showed me how a team's diversity could be its greatest strength. Their cultural and linguistic expertise helped bridge gaps between students, families, and the school, creating an environment where everyone felt understood and valued. I realized that each of us brought unique skills to the table, and together, we could offer students a more comprehensive support system.

Later, Ms. K introduced me to Ms. G, another assistant who had been with the school for six years. Ms. G, originally from Mexico, was fluent in Spanish, which was invaluable since many of our students came from low-income Hispanic families. This interaction made me reflect on the importance of having a diverse teaching staff to meet the needs of the diverse student population. By working closely with colleagues who shared the students' cultural and linguistic backgrounds, we could more effectively communicate with students and their families, ensuring that everyone felt included and supported.

That day gave me a glimpse of the role I was stepping into. I wasn't just there to teach English; I was becoming part of a team that would support students both academically and personally. I began to see my role not just as an individual educator but as part of a collective effort to uplift and empower our students. By leaning on my colleagues' strengths and sharing my own, I could contribute to a culture of collaboration and support that would benefit every child in our care.

At the end of the day, I reflected on the importance of teamwork and communication within the school environment. Collaboration among teachers, staff, and administrators is essential to creating a learning environment where all students, especially English-language learners, can thrive. At the heart of all this, whether it was the bond between teachers, the trust we built with students, or the connections to their families, was the understanding that relationships are the foundation of education. Without them, learning cannot thrive. This realization solidified my commitment to nurturing those relationships every day, knowing they would be the key to our collective success.

Teacher Tip

The longer I'm in education, the more I realize that it all boils down to the connections we make. Truly getting to know your students, not just their test scores, but who they are. Their names, their backgrounds, the little quirks that make them, well, them. It makes all the difference when a student feels seen, especially those who've spent years feeling like just another face in the crowd. And leaning on your colleagues? Honestly, it's a lifeline. Sharing ideas, admitting when you're struggling, celebrating small wins together build a sense of community that carries you through the hardest days. When the adults in a school support each other, it sets the tone for everyone. But the most powerful thing of all? Believing in those kids. I've seen what that kind of belief can do. A simple, sincere word of encouragement can shift something deep inside a student. As teachers, our belief in our students, our presence, our humanity matters more than we may ever truly know. "Every time I wanted to give up, I remembered what you said: that you saw something in me. No one had ever said that before," said a former student, years after graduation.

Parent Tip

The best support you can give your child at school often starts with something simple, staying connected. Contact their teachers, attend school events when you can, and don't be afraid to ask questions. You know your child better than anyone, and when you share insights about their personality, strengths, or struggles, it helps teachers understand how to support them more effectively. At home, make space for little check-ins. Ask how their day was, and really listen. Even the smallest moments of conversation can reveal how they're feeling about school, friends, and learning. When your child sees that you and their teachers are working together, they feel supported, seen, and encouraged. That kind of partnership sends a powerful message: "You matter. We're in this with you."

3 Fostering Diversity and Inclusion in the Classroom

A week passed, and the first day of school finally arrived. I had spent the night in restless anticipation, waking up every hour to check the alarm clock. Each glance at the time reminded me of the significance of the day ahead. This wasn't just a new teaching job; it was my first step into a role where I would have the privilege of learning as much as I taught. The excitement was palpable, but so were the nerves. Could I live up to the responsibility of helping my students not only learn English but also feel seen, valued, and included?

At 5 a.m., unable to stay in bed any longer, I decided to start my day. The early morning stillness offered a brief moment of calm, my "me time." I cherished this ritual as a way to prepare myself mentally and emotionally, knowing that each day in the classroom would bring its own challenges and triumphs. After preparing breakfast, packing lunch boxes, and dropping my children off at the nearby middle school, I drove to the elementary school where my teaching journey was about to officially begin.

Walking into the school, I was handed my new ID badge. As I clipped it onto my shirt, I felt a surge of pride and responsibility. It was more than just a piece of plastic; it symbolized my new role as an educator and the trust the school had placed in me to make a difference. Ms. K greeted me warmly in her classroom, her kindness immediately putting me at ease. Together, we headed to the cafeteria for morning duty, a weekly responsibility that, as she explained, was essential for ensuring students started their day in a safe, structured way.

The cafeteria was a hive of activity as students filed in, chatting with friends and searching for their seats. We stood by the entrance, handing out name cards as students introduced themselves. It was a seemingly small task, but it quickly became clear how meaningful it was. Learning and using a student's name is one of the simplest yet most powerful ways to show them they matter.

For English learners, whose identities are often tied closely to their names, this moment of connection can be transformative. It sets the tone for trust and belonging, critical elements for students who are navigating the challenges of a new language and culture.

After morning duty, Ms. K explained the school's ESOL program, which followed a pull-out model. In this approach, English learners were taken out of their regular classrooms for part of the day to receive focused language instruction in smaller groups. This setup provided a safe space where students could practice their English skills without fear of judgment, gradually building their confidence. I appreciated how this method allowed us to meet students' unique needs while still integrating them into the larger school community. Research confirms that small-group instruction improves outcomes for English learners, as it offers the individualized attention they need to thrive. I was eager to see how this model would unfold in practice.

As we walked through the bustling hallways, I couldn't help but feel inspired by the diversity of the students around me. This wasn't just a job about teaching English; it was about creating a space where every student felt valued and respected, regardless of their background.

In a classroom filled with students from different cultures and experiences, inclusion isn't just an ideal—it's a necessity. When students feel they belong, they are more likely to take risks, engage with their learning, and achieve their potential. I realized that fostering this sense of community would be at the heart of my work.

In the classroom, I observed Ms. K masterfully embody this philosophy. Her teaching style blended structure with creativity, ensuring that every student, regardless of their English proficiency, felt included. She was a natural at differentiated instruction, tailoring lessons to meet students at their level while challenging them to grow. One lesson in particular stood out as a perfect example of her approach.

Ms. K stood in front of the class and announced, "I have a sound in my mind, and I want you to guess it." She wrote three words on the board—cat, fat, and mat—and read them aloud.

"These words all have the sound I'm thinking of," she explained, pointing to the word fit and adding, "But this word does not." The students leaned forward, their curiosity piqued. Ms. K handed each of them a card and asked them to write down their guesses.

One by one, the students figured out the short "a" sound, their faces lighting up with pride as they held up their answers. This discovery-based approach encouraged critical thinking and active participation, key components of language acquisition. By allowing the students to uncover the sound pattern themselves, Ms. K promoted higher order thinking skills and gave them a sense of ownership over their learning. It didn't matter where they came from or how fluent their English was—every student was engaged and excited.

The lesson didn't end there. Ms. K handed out simple books filled with short words and asked the students to circle those containing the short "a" sound. Watching the students eagerly dive into the activity, I saw how her thoughtful scaffolding, introducing the concept through discovery and reinforcing it with practice, built their confidence step by step.

This gradual release of responsibility is especially effective for English learners, as it provides the structured support they need while empowering them to work independently.

By the end of the day, I felt both energized and humbled. Ms. K's ability to balance creativity with structure, and her commitment to inclusion, was a masterclass in effective teaching. She reminded me that education is about more than imparting knowledge, it's about creating an environment where every student feels capable, supported, and inspired to succeed. As I reflected on the day, I realized that this journey wasn't just about teaching; it was about learning how to build a community where every child, regardless of their background or abilities, could thrive.

In another lesson, Ms. K brought apples to class—green, red, and yellow—and used them as a creative way to teach about differences and similarities. She encouraged the students to describe the apples, from their colors and shapes to their tastes. The students were invited to touch, smell, and taste the apples, turning the lesson into a sensory-rich experience.

This simple but effective activity wasn't just about apples; it was about teaching diversity in a way that was accessible to young learners. Ms. K subtly conveyed that, just like the apples, people may look different on the outside but still have valuable things to contribute. This activity illustrated how teaching through real-world, hands-on experiences can make abstract concepts more concrete. For English learners, sensory experiences provide additional pathways to understanding, helping bridge the language gap and making lessons more memorable. Through this hands-on activity, students learned that diversity should be celebrated, not just acknowledged. The lesson's message was clear: we all bring something unique to the classroom, and it's those differences that make our learning environment richer.

Lunchtime with the team proved to be an invaluable learning opportunity, offering insights into my new surroundings and the dynamics of the American education system. During these informal gatherings, Ms. K, in her ingenious way, brought together the diverse members of her team, fostering a sense of community and collaboration. For me, this time was more than just a break; it was a chance to observe, listen, and absorb the nuances of the school environment.

One lunchtime, Ms. K shared her story of meeting her husband, an Iranian man, despite her parents' objections. As I listened, I could see that she understood firsthand the challenges of navigating a relationship that crosses cultural and religious boundaries. It was a beautiful reminder that our differences do not divide us but rather offer opportunities to connect on a deeper level.

Similarly, Ms. C spoke about Hanukkah, explaining how she and her family celebrated this important Jewish holiday. Her detailed account of lighting the menorah each night, one candle at a time, touched me, revealing the deep roots of tradition and the way these customs connect us to our past. Listening to Ms. C describe her family's traditions made me realize how important it was to acknowledge and celebrate the unique backgrounds each student brought into the classroom.

Ms. G's stories of her Mexican heritage were equally enlightening. Her honesty about the struggles her family faced opened my eyes to the complexities that many students bring with them. When she shared the story of her son's friend being beaten up, simply for walking with a white girl, her words struck a chord, leaving me with a deep sense of sadness and urgency. It was a stark reminder that, despite the progress that was made, there were still barriers to inclusion that many of our students faced outside the safety of our school walls.

Sharing lunch with the team became a valuable opportunity to learn about my new environment and better understand the workings of the American education system. During these informal gatherings, Ms. K, my mentor, brought together the diverse members of her team in her ingenious way, fostering a sense of community and collaboration. For me, this time was more than just a break; it was a chance to observe, listen, and absorb the nuances of the school environment.

One of the things that truly brought us closer was sharing food. I still remember the first time I tasted homemade tamales, a dish lovingly prepared by Ms. G. It was my first time trying tamales, and the flavors were unlike anything I had tasted before, rich, comforting, and filled with tradition. In return, I was excited to share a piece of my own culture with the team by bringing Egyptian food that I had cooked. Preparing and sharing dishes like koshari and stuffed grape leaves gave me a chance to introduce them to flavors from my own background, and it was heartwarming to see their genuine interest and appreciation.

Our shared meals went beyond just satisfying our hunger, they became a symbol of the mutual respect and curiosity we had for one another's cultures. It was through these simple acts of sharing that I began to feel more at ease, not just as part of the team but as someone who was contributing to its rich cultural tapestry. Just as sharing food brought our team closer, I realized that sharing and celebrating our students' diverse cultural backgrounds could strengthen their sense of belonging in the classroom. These lunchtime conversations were not merely about exchanging stories; they were moments of genuine connection, empathy, and learning.

As these bonds began to form, I realized that I was flourishing in an environment that embraced diversity and inclusion. It wasn't just about theory anymore, these were lived experiences, unfolding in front of me. The United States had proven to be a place where anyone, regardless of background, could develop and thrive if they were ready to work hard and learn. I was starting to feel more at ease at my main campus, and much of that ease came from these lunchtime gatherings, where respect and openness naturally fostered personal growth. Through these shared experiences, I discovered that inclusion was the foundation upon which I could build my own success.

By the end of the day, I reflected on how essential it was to embrace the diversity within our school community. Ms. K's approach to teaching wasn't just about academics, it was about creating a learning environment where every student felt confident and proud of who they were.

When we make students' cultural and linguistic backgrounds part of the curriculum, we validate their experiences and create a classroom culture where every student is valued. Research shows that culturally responsive teaching practices, like those modeled by Ms. K, improve student engagement, motivation, and academic achievement. By valuing each student's background and incorporating it into the lessons, she built a classroom culture that celebrated differences while fostering connection.

I left school that day with a renewed sense of purpose. I knew that my role wasn't just to teach English; it was to help create an environment where every student felt they belonged, and where their unique contributions were recognized and valued. Through Ms. K's example, I realized that inclusivity and diversity were not just concepts—they were practices that, when embraced, could transform the classroom into a place of growth for everyone.

Teacher Tip

When you stand at the front of a classroom, what really hits you is this incredible mix of young people. Each one sees the world through their own lens, and has their own way of clicking with what you're trying to teach. For me, one of the most rewarding parts of this job—truly, one of the biggest joys—is figuring out how to connect with each of them, how to be flexible and really see what they need. Differentiated instruction? It sounds academic, but it's really just about opening your eyes and realizing that every single kid walks in with a whole universe of experiences and ideas. Our job is to meet them where they are.

I remember early in my career, I stumbled upon inductive teaching almost by accident. Instead of just laying down the rules, I'd pose a question, show them some examples, and let them puzzle it out together.

The energy in the room when they started making those connections themselves? It was electric. You could see the "aha!" moments dawning on their faces. It wasn't just about learning facts; they were building their own understanding.

And for our students who are still finding their way with English, you have to get creative. Words can be so abstract. But if you bring in real objects, use pictures, get them moving, suddenly, those concepts become tangible and abstract ideas become concrete.

I've seen kids go from being completely lost to having this breakthrough, just by holding something in their hands or seeing it visually. It's like unlocking a door for them.

Scaffolding is another one that's become so important in my teaching. Sometimes a task just looks like this huge mountain to climb. But if you break it down into smaller, manageable steps, and you're there to guide them at each stage, slowly letting them take over … it's amazing to watch their confidence blossom. They start to believe in their own abilities.

But maybe the most profound shift in my teaching has been realizing the power of simply trying to understand my students' lives outside of school. You don't need to be an expert on every culture, not at all. It's more about creating a space where their stories, their traditions, their perspectives are valued. When a student feels seen, truly seen, and respected for who they are, the walls come down. They engage more deeply, and honestly, that feeling of belonging? It changes everything. It transforms not just their learning, but the whole dynamic of the classroom. "It reminds you why you got into teaching in the first place."

How does that feel now? I've tried to use more personal anecdotes ("early in my career," "I remember"), more informal language ("puzzle it out," "electric," "aha!"), and a more reflective tone, as if a teacher is sharing their journey and insights.

Parent Tip

When I used to ask my sons, "How was your day?" The answer was almost always the same: "Good." And that was it. I realized they weren't being distant, they just didn't know how to answer something so open-ended.

Over time, I learned that the key is to ask **specific** questions that give kids something concrete to respond to. Here are a few that helped open up real conversations:

"What was the best part of your day today?"
"Was there anything that confused you in class?"
"Who did you spend time with at recess or lunch?"

These kinds of questions do more than get answers, they build trust. They show your child that you care about the details of their world, and they help create a habit of open, ongoing communication about school life.

4 Teaching Experiences Across Two Campuses

By the time my second week as a paraprofessional rolled around, I was beginning to find my rhythm, navigating the unique challenges of working across two very different campuses. Although the schools were located on the same road, they represented two contrasting worlds.

The northern campus primarily served students from low socio-economic backgrounds, while the southern campus catered to families in a more affluent neighborhood. These differences became a lens through which I gained invaluable insights into the diversity of student needs, and the role educators play in bridging these divides.

My mornings began at the northern campus, where limited resources and significant challenges outside of school were part of daily life for many students. Yet, as I greeted each child at the door, I saw something remarkable: resilience. No matter what they faced at home, the students approached school with curiosity and a hunger to learn. One student, Maria, would often arrive late, her uniform slightly rumpled and her backpack nearly empty. Yet, the moment lessons began, her eyes lit up with determination. She reminded me that, for some children, school is more than just a place to learn, it's a sanctuary of stability and hope.

In the afternoons, I stepped into an entirely different world at the southern campus. Here, classrooms were vibrant and brimming with resources. Students arrived with the latest gadgets, pristine backpacks, and colorful school supplies. The privilege of abundance was evident in every corner, from the state-of-the-art technology to the well-stocked libraries. Yet, despite these stark contrasts, one thing became clear: the universal love of learning. Whether at the northern or southern campus, students shared the same desire to grow, explore, and succeed. This realization stayed with me, reinforcing my belief that every child, regardless of circumstance, deserves the tools and opportunities to thrive.

One afternoon at the southern campus, I observed a math teacher whose classroom organization left me in awe. Her room was a masterclass in efficiency. Every item, from manipulatives to textbooks, had a designated place, and students moved seamlessly to retrieve and return materials without disrupting the lesson. During one session, she introduced the concept of multiplication using small cubes. Each student physically grouped the cubes into sets, seeing firsthand how multiplication worked as repeated addition. Watching their faces light up with understanding was a revelation. The teacher's structured system not only encouraged independence but also created an environment where students could take ownership of their learning.

The way she seamlessly integrated realia into her lessons demonstrated how effective hands-on learning could be. Manipulatives weren't just supplementary tools, but rather central to the learning experience. Whether students were using counters to solve problems or blocks to build patterns, every tool served a clear purpose, empowering them to make connections between abstract concepts and the tangible world around them.

At the northern campus, I saw a similar approach, though adapted to a resource-limited environment. One teacher used everyday items like apples, coins, and small objects to teach basic math concepts such as addition and subtraction. During one lesson, she handed out apples to her students and asked them to remove a few, demonstrating subtraction in a way that was simple and accessible. For students who often struggled with abstract ideas, these physical representations made the learning process more tangible. It showed me that creativity and intentionality could overcome even the greatest resource gaps.

While the methods at the two campuses differed, the core principle remained the same: students learn best when lessons feel real and relevant. At the northern campus, visual aids were also a cornerstone of instruction, helping to break down complex ideas into manageable parts. For English learners especially, these tools were invaluable, connecting language to meaning in a way that words alone could not. Observing how both schools adapted their teaching styles to meet the unique needs of their students was a lesson in itself. It reinforced the idea that there is no one-size-fits-all approach to education, only the commitment to understanding and addressing the needs of each child.

Throughout my time at both campuses, I found that building relationships was the foundation of effective teaching. One afternoon at the southern campus, I worked with a student struggling with a division problem. I grabbed some counters and grouped them into sets, breaking the problem into smaller, manageable parts. Slowly, the solution unfolded before him. As his face lit up with confidence, I was reminded of the power of patience and encouragement. These small moments of connection had the potential to transform a student's confidence and motivation.

Beyond the classroom, I also developed meaningful relationships with my colleagues. At the southern campus, Ms. Chang, the ESL teacher, shared a Chinese New Year tradition with me, gifting my sons red envelopes filled with money. This simple gesture reminded me of the importance of cultural exchange, not just with students but also among the staff. These moments of mutual respect and shared experiences created a sense of community that enriched the learning environment for everyone.

Looking back, my time at these two campuses was a journey of discovery, not just about teaching methods, but about the power of creating inclusive, supportive spaces for learning. Whether it was the highly structured classrooms of the southern campus or the resourceful creativity of the northern campus, each setting reinforced the importance of adaptability, connection, and intention in education.

The use of manipulatives and realia stood out as particularly impactful tools, bridging the gap between abstract concepts and real-world understanding. These experiences taught me that education is about more than delivering content; it's about creating an environment where students can explore, experiment, and grow. It's about helping them see their own potential, no matter their circumstances. Whether through a kind word, a creative lesson, or a well-organized classroom, educators have the power to make a lasting difference in the lives of every student they meet.

Teacher Tip

One of my go-to moves when a lesson just isn't landing—when I see that look in my students' eyes that says, "I'm not really following this" is to bring in something real. Even with high schoolers, having a physical object they can see or touch often makes abstract ideas click in a way that words alone can't.

I remember reading a passage with my class that described different types of spices, cinnamon, turmeric, cardamom, and I realized most of my students had never encountered some of these before. How could they truly grasp the meaning without a sensory reference? So the next day, I brought in a few spices from home, each in a small plastic bag. We passed them around, smelled each one, and guessed what dishes they might be used in. It completely changed the energy in the room. Suddenly, the words on the page made sense because now they had something real to connect them to.

It reminded me just how powerful realia can be, especially when working with English learners. A simple object can bridge the gap between unfamiliar vocabulary and lived experience, turning confusion into connection, and even sparking meaningful conversations about culture, food, and identity.

Parent Tip

Learning doesn't just live in the classroom, it's woven into everyday life, often in the tiniest moments. Ever counted coins together while cleaning out your purse? Or had your child group fruit by color while unpacking groceries? Even measuring flour for cookies turns into a mini math lesson (with a sweet reward at the end!).

These aren't just chores; they're chances to show your child that what they learn at school means something. It's not just about passing tests; it's about making sense of the world around them. And when they start to connect those dots, you'll see their confidence grow. Their eyes light up, and suddenly they're asking questions, noticing patterns, wanting to try things on their own. That kind of curiosity? It's gold.

5 Stepping into the Teacher's Role

The summer before my first year as a teacher felt like a whirlwind. I had transitioned from being a paraprofessional to a part-time classroom teacher at a middle school, bringing with it excitement, anticipation, and a healthy dose of anxiety. Now, even in a part-time capacity, the responsibility of shaping young minds rested squarely on my shoulders.

Before the school year began, I attended two full days of staff development. The sessions covered a wide range of topics, from teaching strategies to classroom management techniques, and even icebreakers for the first week of school. One session introduced me to effective questioning strategies to engage students, like asking open-ended questions that encouraged discussion, while another focused on creating a positive classroom culture from day one. These professional development days helped me structure my lessons and build relationships with my students, skills I would soon find essential in my first week of teaching. During a break, a brief conversation with a seasoned teacher left a lasting impression on me. She said, "Stay away from negative people." I've come to understand how true that is, while everyone can have a rough day now and then, if someone seems to be having a bad day every single day, perhaps it's time they reconsider whether teaching is still the right fit. That advice helped me stay grounded and seek out positive, supportive colleagues in those early weeks.

On the first day of school, I introduced myself: "Good morning, everyone. I'm Ms. El-Baz." The quiet room soon filled with curious eyes, and I knew this was the start of something significant. As I looked around the room, I could see both curiosity and nervousness reflected back at me. Breaking the ice wasn't easy, but as students began to introduce themselves, I started to see their personalities emerge. This was my first time leading a classroom on my own, and while I felt prepared, I also knew that this journey would be filled with both challenges and growth.

From the outset, I wanted my classroom to be a welcoming space. I decorated it with a poster that said "Welcome" in multiple languages, symbolizing the diverse backgrounds of my students. Items around the room, such as staplers and rulers, were labeled, allowing students to feel comfortable and independent navigating the space. These small efforts made the classroom feel like it belonged to all of us and were important first steps in creating an inclusive environment.

However, I quickly realized that creating a welcoming space was only part of the challenge. In an ESL classroom, learners come from different cultures and backgrounds, and at times, they may not be fully prepared for the diversity they encounter. This can lead to misunderstandings or even teasing, particularly around differences in language proficiency and pronunciation. Early on, I noticed some students making fun of each other's accents or pronunciation. I knew I had to address this directly.

I made it a priority to set clear expectations from the very beginning: negative remarks or jokes about pronunciation would not be tolerated. We were all learning together, and it was my job to ensure that the learning environment remained safe for everyone. I reminded my students that the classroom was a space where mistakes were part of the learning process, and no one should feel embarrassed or hesitant to speak. Whenever a student forgot this rule, I would gently but firmly remind them that respect was nonnegotiable in our classroom.

This simple, consistent message helped create an environment where students felt comfortable practicing their language skills without fear of judgment. Over time, I saw them begin to support one another, helping their peers through difficult pronunciations and celebrating each other's progress. One day, I watched as two students worked together during a speaking activity. One struggled with the word "through," and the other patiently broke the word into syllables, repeating it until they got it right. Moments like this showed me that learning was not just about mastering a language but also about building a community of support.

Looking back, I realized that teaching isn't just about delivering lessons, rather, it's about creating a space where students feel seen, respected, and empowered to grow. While my first days were filled with challenges, they were also the foundation for some of the most rewarding experiences of my career.

During my first year, I attended a CHAMPS training provided by the school district, which became a turning point in my approach to classroom management. The training took place in an open-space elementary school where classrooms had no walls, yet students worked quietly and productively in a safe, focused atmosphere. Referred to as "CHAMPS Campus," it was an eye-opener for me. The level of discipline, respect, and focus these students displayed showed me just how powerful structured behavioral systems could be.

The CHAMPS system is an acronym that stands for Conversation, Help, Activity, Movement, Participation, and Success. Each letter represents a key component of expected student behavior:

- **C** stands for **Conversation**: Can students talk during this activity? If so, at what voice level and with whom?
- **H** stands for **Help**: How do students get assistance if they need it?
- **A** is for **Activity**: What is the task or objective students should be working on?
- **M** stands for **Movement**: Are students allowed to move about, and under what conditions?
- **P** is for **Participation**: What does active and appropriate participation look like?
- **S** is for **Success**, which is the result of following all the expectations consistently.

These clear and structured expectations helped students understand how to behave in various scenarios, from group work to independent study. What stood out most to me was the consistency with which CHAMPS was implemented across the entire school. The system wasn't limited to individual classrooms; it extended to common areas like the cafeteria, hallways, and library. This consistency created a unified culture of respect and responsibility throughout the school. Students always knew what was expected of them, whether they were eating lunch, transitioning between classes, or sitting in a lesson.

After witnessing the success of CHAMPS, I implemented many of its strategies in my own classroom. I began by defining clear expectations for each type of classroom activity, ensuring my students knew how to behave in different scenarios. This not only helped manage classroom behavior but also empowered my students to take responsibility for their actions. Rather than constantly reminding them to stay on task or lower their voices, I used the CHAMPS model to help them understand what was expected at all times.

To support my English language learners, I created a CHAMPS expectations poster using **visuals** and **simplified language**. This helped make the expectations more accessible and reinforced the structure they needed to thrive. Over time, this system fostered a greater sense of independence among my students, and the classroom atmosphere became more conducive to learning.

While CHAMPS gave me the tools to create a structured and respectful environment, I quickly realized that classroom management was only part of the equation. Preparing engaging lessons and setting clear academic expectations were equally critical, especially when teaching English language learners (ELs). As I worked to create a positive learning space, I found myself reflecting on how to make my lessons not just organized, but meaningful and accessible to my students.

Once a structured environment was in place, I turned my attention to supporting students in more complex academic tasks, especially those requiring higher-level language skills. I quickly realized the textbook alone wasn't enough to engage my students or meet their diverse needs. It became clear I needed to move beyond traditional methods and incorporate dynamic, student-centered strategies to make learning more interactive.

This need became especially evident as I observed the gap between conversational fluency and academic language skills. I had read about the distinction between Basic Interpersonal Communication Skills (BICS) and Cognitive Academic Language Proficiency (CALP), but it wasn't until I stepped into the classroom that I truly grasped its significance. Many of my students could hold casual conversations within a year or two, but the language of essays, exams, and critical thinking was a far greater hurdle. Academic language required intentional planning, scaffolding, and creative ways to make complex ideas accessible.

I remember one day, an eighth-grade science teacher approached me, clearly frustrated. She had overheard one of our students chatting fluently in English with a friend in the hallway, but in her class, he barely spoke and acted like he didn't understand. Right away, I recognized the issue; she was witnessing the difference between BICS and CALP, even if she didn't know the terminology. I gently explained that sounding fluent in everyday conversation doesn't mean a student is ready to navigate academic content.

To support my students, I began explicitly teaching academic language. I focused on signal words like "because," "however," and "therefore" to help students build logical connections, and I introduced content-specific vocabulary to give them the tools they needed to participate meaningfully in class discussions and readings. It wasn't about capability; it was about giving them the language to show what they knew.

I also encouraged my students to answer in complete sentences and to incorporate academic terms in their responses. This helped reinforce their understanding while preparing them for more formal writing. Over time, I saw their confidence grow as they began expressing themselves more clearly in both speech and writing.

That first year in the classroom taught me lessons I carry with me to this day. From building a respectful, inclusive culture to implementing behavior systems like CHAMPS, I learned that a successful learning environment demands both careful planning and flexibility. Most of all, it requires seeing each student as an individual—with their own stories, struggles, and strengths. As my journey continued, I held tight to these lessons, always striving to create a space where every learner felt seen, supported, and capable of success.

Teacher Tip

A smooth start sets the tone for the whole year. That's why I always begin by clearly showing students what respect, kindness, and good learning habits look like, whether we're doing group work, listening to a lesson, or walking down the hallway.

Tools like CHAMPS help me guide students through what's expected in different parts of the day. But just as important as routines is the classroom culture. I make sure every child feels seen and valued, especially in a diverse classroom where many students are on their own language journey. We celebrate their progress together, and I gently but consistently stop teasing or exclusion in its tracks. When students feel safe and respected, they're more likely to grow, not just academically, but socially too.

Parent Tip

At home, you can help keep that positive momentum going. Talk to your child about what it means to be kind and respectful to classmates, especially those who are still learning English or speak with a different accent. Remind them that no one learns without making mistakes, and that the best way to support their peers is by helping and encouraging them, not by making fun of them. As a bilingual family, you already know how powerful language can be. Help your child see their classmates' differences as something to value, not something to avoid. Everyone learns in their own way, and a little patience and kindness can make a big difference. When kids hear this message both at school and at home, they grow into thoughtful, inclusive friends and learners.

Part 2
Bridging Cultures and Emotions in the Classroom

6 Connecting Hearts and Minds

As the school year came to a close during my first year in 2007, the state test results finally arrived. While not all of my students passed, their remarkable progress was a testament to their hard work and determination. I couldn't have been prouder. This achievement wouldn't have been possible without the unwavering support of my colleagues, school principals, and district administrators, who guided me and provided invaluable resources throughout the year. Recognizing the progress my students made, the school principal walked into my classroom one afternoon with a warm smile and said, "You've done an amazing job." Then, to my surprise, she offered me a full-time position for the next school year.

I could hardly contain my excitement. This was the moment I had been working so hard for, and it felt incredible to have my efforts recognized. A full-time role would allow me to connect even more deeply with my students, parents, and colleagues, and I was eager to continue making a difference. Yet, with this recognition came new challenges. I knew that stepping into this role meant greater responsibilities, not just maintaining my students' progress, but finding new ways to reach those who were still struggling. The lingering question, "Could I do even better next year?" became my motivation as I embraced this opportunity with determination and a renewed sense of purpose.

Having my own classroom allowed me to strengthen the relationships I was beginning to build. I made it a point to attend my students' after-school activities, such as concerts, sports events, and talent shows. Each time they spotted me in the audience, their faces lit up with joy and excitement. It was in those moments that I realized how much my presence outside the classroom meant to them. Teaching was about more than just lessons; rather, it was about showing students they mattered as individuals.

One student, who had been shy and reserved, started opening up more after I attended her soccer game. She began sharing stories about her team and participating more in class discussions, her confidence growing with every interaction. Another memorable moment came with Thu, a student who hardly spoke any English when the school year began. After attending a school concert where he played the violin, he approached me the next day with a big smile and said, "I saw you yesterday." He thanked me for being there, and I praised his beautiful performance, telling him how impressed I was with his talent. From that day forward, Thu's transformation was remarkable. He began to communicate and interact more in class, raising his hand to answer questions and eagerly sharing his thoughts during group discussions. These moments reminded me of how small gestures of support could create a ripple effect, helping students feel seen, valued, and confident.

Watching my students perform, compete, and interact with their peers revealed different sides of their personalities, talents, and challenges. Seeing a quiet student shine during a talent show taught me the importance of creating opportunities for every child to succeed. These insights changed how I approached teaching. I began tailoring lessons to connect with their interests and strengths, weaving what I learned about them into our classroom activities. Being present in their world helped me become a more effective teacher in mine.

While building rapport with students' parents, many of whom were, like me when I first arrived in the United States, unfamiliar with the American education system, I realized how important it was to involve them in their children's learning journey. One day, a parent of a high-achieving student questioned why her son received full marks despite several grammar and spelling mistakes.

"I noticed my son made several grammar mistakes," she said. "Shouldn't his grade be lower?"

"That's a great observation," I replied. "In this assignment, we focused on developing ideas rather than perfect grammar. Your son's creativity was outstanding."

Her eyes lit up with understanding, and she proudly praised her son. This interaction made me realize how crucial it was to help parents understand the grading system and engage them in their child's progress.

Inspired by a fellow ESL teacher who had organized a parents' night for English learners to explain their classwork in their native languages, I decided to create similar opportunities for parents to feel included and informed, regardless of language barriers. At one event, a father shared that understanding the grading criteria gave him confidence to encourage his daughter at home. These efforts not only engaged families but also empowered students to take ownership of their learning. Strengthening the home–school connection became a vital part of my teaching philosophy.

At the same time, I was reflecting more deeply on how to tailor my instruction within the classroom to meet my students' individual needs. One concept that transformed my approach was recognizing and addressing different learning styles. I realized that each student had a unique way of processing information, and adapting my teaching methods to these preferences could maximize their engagement and comprehension. For visual learners, I incorporated charts, videos, and graphic organizers. For auditory learners, I emphasized class discussions, verbal explanations, and opportunities to listen to others' perspectives. For kinesthetic learners, I incorporated hands-on activities, role-playing, and experiments that brought lessons to life.

One memorable moment was during a math lesson when I used fraction tiles as manipulatives. A student who had struggled with abstract concepts lit up when he could physically move the pieces to solve problems. He exclaimed, "Oh, now I get it!" I also noticed that students were more engaged overall, with even struggling learners showing increased interest. Understanding their learning styles didn't just help me in the classroom, but it allowed me to communicate more effectively with their parents. I could explain why certain approaches worked better for their child and suggest ways to support their learning at home. These connections enriched the learning experience for students and strengthened their confidence.

These experiences marked a turning point in my teaching journey. I was no longer just an observer or participant; I was actively contributing to the growth and understanding of the school community. Collaborating with colleagues to share insights and strategies became a source of inspiration and growth. I realized that connecting hearts and minds wasn't just about addressing academic struggles or achievements, but it was about fostering a sense of belonging in the classroom and beyond. Whether it was engaging students through meaningful activities, partnering with parents to support their children's growth, or collaborating with colleagues, each connection built a stronger, more engaged learning environment.

Teacher Tip

A strong classroom begins with strong connections. Before focusing on academic outcomes, invest time in building rapport with students, their families, and your colleagues. Use tools like CHAMPS to establish a positive and structured environment, and then adapt your instruction to match students' learning styles. Pay attention to how they respond to visuals, movement, or discussion, and adjust your approach accordingly. Even small gestures, such as attending a student's performance or helping a parent understand classroom expectations, can strengthen trust and encourage engagement. When students feel supported and understood, they become more confident, motivated, and ready to learn.

Parent Tip

Take time to ask your child about their favorite part of the school day or something new they learned. Simple questions like, "What did you enjoy most in class today?" or "Is there something you're still curious about?" show your interest in their learning and encourage them to reflect on their progress.

Additionally, stay informed about the classroom activities and grading criteria by attending parent–teacher meetings or events. If your child is an English learner, don't hesitate to ask for explanations in your preferred language when needed. Building this bridge with your child's teacher helps you better support your child's learning journey at home.

7 Empowering Diversity Through Cultural Sensitivity

Creating a positive classroom isn't just about fixing grammar mistakes or following the curriculum to the letter. It's about making sure every student feels like they truly belong, that who they are and where they come from matter. While we work hard to help students find their voice in writing, we also need to make space for their real-life stories, their cultures, and their experiences to be seen and respected.

That means going beyond simply acknowledging their home languages or holiday traditions. It means understanding how their past schooling, family expectations, and cultural values shape the way they learn, and then adjusting our teaching to meet them where they are.

Research has shown time and again that when students see themselves reflected in what they're learning, they're more engaged and motivated. For students who are new to a country or who come from marginalized communities, this is especially powerful. It tells them: you matter here. And when students feel that kind of connection, they're more likely to grow, take risks, and take charge of their learning.

I remember one student in particular, Sara, who had just moved from Saudi Arabia. She was trying to find her place in a new culture while staying true to the values her family held dear. She was smart and eager, but often torn between what she wanted and what was expected of her at home. I knew that helping her succeed wasn't just about giving her academic support, but it was about building trust.

One afternoon, her father came in for a parent meeting and shared his worries about some of the classroom activities. He was respectful, but concerned. I listened carefully, let him know I understood, and worked with him to find ways for Sara to participate without going against her family's values. I also had a quiet chat with Sara, giving her space to talk about the pressure she felt and what she hoped for. Together, we came up with a plan that worked for both her and her family. That experience reminded me that when we truly partner with families and show respect for their values, we create stronger support systems for our students.

Being culturally responsive also means weaving students' cultures into our everyday teaching. Whether it's reading books that reflect their experiences, bringing their stories into class discussions, or designing projects that let them celebrate their heritage, these moments tell students: your story belongs here too. In one project, I asked students to bring in something from their culture, a recipe, a tradition, even a family saying, and explain its meaning. The classroom lit up with pride and curiosity as students taught each other about their worlds. It was one of those rare moments where learning felt effortless, joyful, and deeply human.

That's the heart of culturally responsive teaching; it's not about grand gestures, but about creating a classroom where every student feels seen, heard, and valued. When we do that, we don't just teach them academics. We teach them that they belong.

Building trust with families isn't just a good teaching strategy, but it's also the heart of culturally sensitive education. It starts with a simple step: reaching out. Early in the school year, I make it a point to connect with parents, not just to talk about grades or behavior, but to learn about their hopes, values, and expectations. That small gesture, just listening, goes a long way. When families feel seen and respected, they're more likely to get involved, and that connection can make all the difference in a student's experience.

One moment that stands out is when Sara's father became our LPAC parent representative. He wasn't just attending meetings; he was helping us bridge two worlds: school and home. His involvement made Sara feel supported, and it reminded me how powerful it is when families become true partners in their child's learning.

Sometimes, we need to go beyond words and show families that their culture matters in the classroom. One year, I invited students to bring in family artifacts or photos and create a "Culture Corner." You could feel the pride in the room as students shared stories behind their objects. It wasn't just a bulletin board; it became a living reminder that every background had a place in our classroom story.

Of course, teaching isn't just about relationships, it's also about helping students adapt to new ways of learning. Many ELs come from schools where the teacher lectures and students listen. When I first asked my students to work in groups or talk with a partner, some looked at me like I was speaking a different language, not because of English, but because the whole idea was unfamiliar.

So we started small. I introduced "think-pair-share," explained why we were doing it, and showed how it helped build real-life skills like communication and critical thinking. Bit by bit, they warmed up. The key was always to explain the why and to make space for mistakes and growth.

One student, Victor, taught me just how important this process can be. Victor had recently moved from Vietnam and was laser-focused on becoming an engineer. He preferred working alone and didn't see the point in group work. In his mind, independence equaled success.

Instead of pushing him, I sat down with him and asked about his goals. When he mentioned engineering, I gently pointed out how often engineers work in teams—on designs, prototypes, and real-world problem-solving. He paused, nodded, and admitted he wasn't used to collaborating in class.

So I met him halfway. I started by pairing him with just one other student who also loved math and science. They worked on a challenge that felt like something out of an engineering lab, building a structure using limited materials. It wasn't about the perfect solution, but it was about learning to bounce ideas off each other. Slowly, Victor got more comfortable. I gradually increased the group size and complexity of the tasks, always tying them back to his dream of becoming an engineer.

Managing a culturally diverse classroom also means understanding how students interpret authority and structure. In some cultures, students are used to formal relationships with teachers, where speaking up or challenging ideas isn't encouraged. Knowing this, I made sure to keep clear routines and expectations while modeling how to respectfully share ideas and ask questions.

I even taught discussion skills explicitly such as how to raise your hand, how to listen actively, and how to disagree kindly. It might seem basic, but for many students, these were brand-new concepts. Over time, these lessons created a classroom that balanced structure with openness where students felt both safe and empowered.

In the end, culturally responsive teaching is about meeting students and families where they are and gently guiding them forward. It's about listening, adapting, and showing each student that their voice matters—not just in the classroom, but in the bigger world they're preparing to shape.

To help Victor feel more confident, I provided him with clear roles during group work. For instance, he often took on the role of the team planner, outlining the steps needed to complete the task. This allowed him to contribute meaningfully while still staying within his comfort zone. As he grew more confident, I encouraged him to rotate roles, eventually taking on responsibilities like presenting his group's findings to the class. This step-by-step approach helped Victor feel more secure in interacting with his classmates.

I also made it a point to celebrate his contributions publicly. When Victor successfully collaborated with his team, I praised his efforts in front of the class, reinforcing the value of his input. For example, after a project where Victor's team created a bridge model, I highlighted how his planning skills helped the group succeed. His classmates also began to recognize and appreciate his strengths, which boosted his confidence further.

As Victor became more comfortable working with his peers, I noticed a shift in his attitude. He started to see group activities not just as an academic requirement but as a way to learn from others and share his own knowledge. By connecting collaborative tasks to his personal and career goals, and by scaffolding his participation in group work, I was able to help Victor develop skills that he later acknowledged as essential for his future. His journey underscored the importance of meeting students where they are while gently guiding them toward growth.

Parents also play a crucial role in fostering cultural sensitivity. Encouraging students to share their cultural experiences and perspectives in the classroom not only builds their confidence but also enriches the learning environment for all. For example, a student once shared a traditional folktale from her home country during a storytelling unit. The class was fascinated, and it sparked a lively discussion about the similarities and differences between various cultures' storytelling traditions. This moment highlighted the power of bringing students' cultural backgrounds into the classroom, creating a richer and more inclusive learning experience.

Cultural sensitivity is a powerful tool for creating inclusive classrooms where every student can succeed. By understanding and respecting the diverse educational backgrounds, personal goals, and cultural values that students bring with them, teachers can create a learning environment that empowers all students to reach their full potential. When we embrace diversity as a strength, we create classrooms where students don't just learn—they thrive.

Being intentional about incorporating cultural perspectives into your curriculum is key. Recognize the value of students' prior educational experiences and help them bridge the gap between their previous learning environments and their new classroom. Remember, this work benefits everyone, not just students from diverse backgrounds. By fostering empathy, awareness, and collaboration, we prepare all students to engage with a globalized world.

Teacher Tip

Start the school year by getting to know your students, not just their names and reading levels, but who they are and where they come from. A simple conversation, a short survey, or a welcome activity can open a window into their cultural backgrounds and previous learning experiences. Use what you learn to shape your lessons so that every student sees a bit of themselves in the curriculum. Include stories, songs, or traditions from different cultures, and invite students to share their own when they feel ready. When it's time for group work, take a moment to explain the why and how behind it, so that even those new to this learning style feel comfortable. And don't forget to carve out moments for students to celebrate who they are, whether through projects, storytelling, or simple show-and-tell moments.

When we create a classroom where every culture is welcomed and valued, everyone benefits. We build not only better learners, but also more compassionate human beings.

Parent Tip

As a parent who has lived as a foreigner in many countries, I know how important it is for our children to feel proud of where they come from. One simple way to support that is by sharing a piece of your culture with their school. I remember once baking kunafa and taking it to my sons' classroom. The kids were so curious and excited to try something new. It was a small gesture, but it opened up a whole conversation about traditions, family, and the foods that bring us together. My sons were beaming with pride, and their classmates got to learn something they might never have encountered otherwise.

These moments matter. Whether it's food, a story, a song, or even a family photo, your contributions help your child feel seen and valued, and they help the entire classroom become a more welcoming place.

Don't hesitate to talk to your child's teacher about what's important to your family, or to share any challenges your child may be facing. Teachers truly appreciate that insight and want to support your child as best they can.

Most importantly, remind your child often: their culture, their language, their story, it's not just welcome in the classroom. It's a gift.

Part 3
Teaching Strategies for Language Development

8 Bringing Vocabulary and Culture to Life Through Images

I find in an ESL classroom, language is more than grammar and vocabulary; it's a gateway to understanding cultural contexts and historical backgrounds. By using art, we engage students in conversations about both language and the moments that have shaped societies. Artworks like Norman Rockwell's *The Problem We All Live With* and Margaret Bourke-White's 1937 Great Depression photograph *Breadline During the Louisville Flood* serve as cultural touchstones, encouraging students to explore language within historical and social narratives. Visual art also invites students to develop empathy and engage deeply with stories of resilience, courage, and societal challenges.

Visual art is a powerful tool for developing all four language skills namely, listening, speaking, reading, and writing. When students observe and comment on an image, they practice speaking, even if it's through single-word responses for beginning students. Listening skills are engaged as students hear peers' observations, allowing them to absorb new vocabulary and phrasing. Writing is practiced as students compose responses or reflections, possibly posting them on a platform like Padlet, where they can read and respond to each other's posts. These activities create opportunities for students to interact with language holistically, fostering both confidence and fluency.

For teachers unfamiliar with the artwork, here are brief thumbnail descriptions of the pieces:

- **Norman Rockwell's *The Problem We All Live With***: This painting depicts Ruby Bridges, a young Black girl walking to an all-white school under the protection of federal marshals during the Civil Rights Movement. She is surrounded by graffiti and racial slurs, symbolizing both bravery and tension.

- **Margaret Bourke-White's *Breadline during the Louisville Flood***: This photograph shows African Americans standing in a long line for relief during the Great Depression. Behind them is a billboard with a wealthy white family and the slogan, "World's Highest Standard of Living," emphasizing the contrast between idealized advertising and harsh reality.

To deepen this connection, image grammar bridges the visual and linguistic aspects of communication. Just as artists use color, shape, and composition to convey meaning, writers use vocabulary, sentence structure, and rhythm to create similar effects. For example, viewing Rockwell's painting might inspire students to use language that reflects courage or isolation, while the structured lines in Bourke-White's photograph could prompt words conveying resilience or hardship. Through interpreting visual details and reflecting them in their language, students learn to "paint with words," building expressive and vivid language skills.

In this chapter, you'll explore techniques and strategies for integrating visual arts into your language teaching. From building academic vocabulary and descriptive language to guiding students in crafting personal narratives, this chapter equips you with creative methods to enhance language mastery. Practical examples, adaptable activities, and a detailed lesson plan will show you how to bring visual arts into your classroom in ways that encourage language use, cultural awareness, and self-expression.

Using Images to Build Background Knowledge and Enhance Literacy

Teaching with images has always been one of my favorite ways to build both language skills and empathy in my ESL classroom. This lesson, designed for grades 5–8, is adaptable for all language proficiency levels— beginning, intermediate, and advanced—allowing every student to connect meaningfully to the content. Over the years, I've refined these activities with my co-teacher to help students use iconic images to build background knowledge, expand their vocabulary, and strengthen critical thinking. Using bilingual dictionaries is an integral part of the process, as it empowers students to bridge their learning with their home language. Here's how we've implemented it.

I began this lesson by gathering my students near a large print of Norman Rockwell's *The Problem We All Live With*. Holding it up, I said, "Today, we're going to use this picture to build background knowledge about history and practice new words. This is a picture of a very brave girl named Ruby Bridges. Images like this help us understand important events and talk about them in a new language."

Pointing to Ruby, I asked, "What do you notice in the picture?" The students hesitated at first, but soon began calling out observations like "There are men walking with her," and "She has a book in her hand." As they spoke, I wrote their ideas on a chart under the heading "What We See in the Picture."

My co-teacher joined in, providing more context: "Ruby was the only Black student at an all-white school during the Civil Rights Movement. The men walking with her are protecting her because some people didn't want Ruby to go to that school. She was very brave to do this." Together, we asked, "How do you think Ruby felt walking to school that day?" The students offered ideas like "scared" and "proud," which we added to the chart under the heading "How Ruby Might Feel."

At this point, I introduced key vocabulary—brave, walk, protect, and school. Holding up vocabulary cards with both words and matching pictures, I said, "Let's say these words together: brave, walk, protect, school. These words will help us talk about Ruby's story." Students had the opportunity to use their bilingual dictionaries to look up translations or synonyms. I reminded them, "Take a few minutes to check the words if you're not sure." This ensured all students felt confident moving forward.

The next day, I reviewed our vocabulary and ideas about Ruby Bridges. "Yesterday, we learned about Ruby," I reminded them. "Today, we'll use another image to learn more about history." I displayed Margaret Bourke-White's famous photograph of people waiting in line during the Great Depression. "What do you notice in this picture?" I asked.

The co-teacher encouraged responses, writing down ideas like "people standing," "a long line," and "a sign." Then they explained, "This photo shows people waiting for help during a very hard time called the Great Depression.

Many people didn't have jobs or enough money. The sign in the background shows a happy scene, but the line shows something very different."

We introduced more vocabulary like waiting, line, and help, and used visuals to clarify meanings. For example, we showed a picture of people in line to reinforce waiting. We then asked inference questions: "Why do you think the people are standing in this line?" and "How do you think they feel?" This encouraged students to connect language to emotions and historical realities.

To reinforce grammar, I asked, "What is happening in the picture?" The students practiced using the present progressive, answering, "They are waiting in line." I pointed out key structures like are waiting and wrote them on the board for students to use in later activities.

For the third lesson, students practiced writing their own sentences about the images. I started by reviewing vocabulary and grammar, providing sentence frames on the board:

- Ruby is going to ___.
- The people are waiting because ___.

I modeled a sentence, saying, "Ruby is going to school with brave steps. Does this help you imagine Ruby's walk?" Together, we refined it, adding details like to a new school.

Students wrote sentences about either the Ruby Bridges image or the Great Depression photo, using bilingual dictionaries to support their writing. As they worked, my co-teacher and I circulated, asking questions like "What word could you use to describe the line?" and "What's another way to say went?"

Once students wrote their sentences, they illustrated them. For advanced learners, we encouraged them to write more complex sentences, like "Ruby's brave walk symbolizes resilience in the face of racial segregation."

To deepen understanding, I asked students to imagine themselves as a character in one of the images. "What would you think or feel if you were Ruby or someone in the line during the Great Depression?" I said. Students wrote diary entries, letters, or short dialogues from their chosen perspective. This creative exercise helped them connect emotionally to the historical context while expanding their language skills.

To evaluate student understanding and language development throughout the lesson, I use a combination of tools that assess participation, writing, and oral communication. During discussions, I observe and take notes on which students actively participate and how well they use new vocabulary and respond to questions. For written tasks, I assess sentences and creative writing using a simple rubric, focusing on clarity, vocabulary use, and grammar. For example, I look for whether students write complete and meaningful sentences, such as Ruby is walking to school with the men protecting her, or more advanced sentences like Ruby's brave walk symbolizes her resilience during the Civil Rights Movement. Students' creative tasks, such as diary entries or letters, are assessed for their ability to capture historical context, use new vocabulary, and demonstrate coherent organization. I also use peer feedback sessions where students share their work and give structured feedback using sentence stems like "I like how you described ___" or "You could add more details about ___." During oral activities, such as matching questions and answers or partner discussions, I listen for correct grammar usage, particularly the present progressive, and assess fluency and pronunciation. Finally, students reflect on their learning by writing a short journal entry or response to prompts like "What did I learn from these pictures?" or "Which new words did I use today?" This multifaceted approach ensures that all aspects of language learning—listening, speaking, reading, and writing—are addressed and provides a comprehensive view of student progress.

Reflecting on these lessons, I'm always amazed by how much students grow when they connect language learning to real-world stories and visual art. The co-teacher and I often reminded them, "Images are a powerful way to build knowledge and practice language. When we describe what we see, we grow our vocabulary, grammar, and understanding together." Incorporating tools like bilingual dictionaries and scaffolding activities for all proficiency levels ensures that every student feels included and capable.

Using Images to Teach Academic Vocabulary and Scientific Concepts: Photosynthesis

Collaborating with the science teacher to teach photosynthesis gave us the chance to combine visuals, hands-on activities, and language practice into a single, engaging lesson. As shown in Figure 8.1, we aimed to make this scientific process accessible and meaningful for students at all proficiency levels.

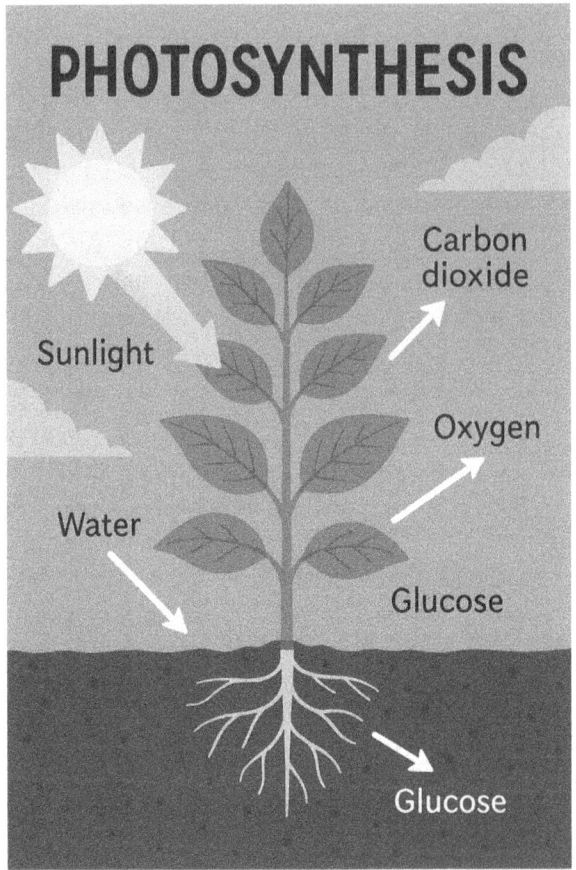

Figure 8.1 A simple illustration demonstrating how photosynthesis works, highlighting key inputs (sunlight, water, carbon dioxide) and outputs (oxygen, glucose). © Created by Nesreen El-Baz.

We began the lesson by introducing a large, labeled diagram showing the steps of photosynthesis.

When teaching the concept of photosynthesis to English learners, the science teacher began by introducing the key idea: "Plants make their own food using sunlight, water, and carbon dioxide." As the explanation unfolded, I supported the lesson by pointing to a diagram showing sunlight, leaves, water, and roots, ensuring that students could visually connect the vocabulary to the concepts being described. To reinforce comprehension, I repeated each key word aloud, inviting students to echo the terms back, which allowed us to focus on accurate pronunciation and recognition. These repetitions created a rhythm in the classroom, helping students internalize both the vocabulary and the scientific process.

To enhance their understanding, I provided sentence frames that connected the vocabulary to the process. I began by modeling examples such as, "Plants need sunlight to make food" and "Plants take in carbon dioxide from the air." Next, students worked in pairs to complete similar sentences, referring to the diagram for guidance. This collaborative practice encouraged peer learning and gave students opportunities to hear and use the language in context. Together, they practiced statements like "Plants take in water through their roots" and "The plant releases oxygen." Using these structured activities, students were able to apply the academic vocabulary in meaningful ways while improving their sentence-building skills.

As the lesson progressed, the science teacher guided students through the steps of photosynthesis, breaking it down into manageable parts: "Sunlight hits the leaves. The plant takes in water. The plant produces oxygen." I took this opportunity to highlight the present tense structures and prepositions being used, such as from and to. To further support their understanding, students used sentence strips to complete statements like "The plant takes in ___" or "The plant produces ___," filling in the blanks with terms like "carbon dioxide" and "oxygen." This hands-on activity helped solidify their grasp of both the science content and the academic language.

For advanced students, we extended the lesson by exploring how photosynthesis impacts agriculture and the environment. The science teacher posed a thought-provoking question: "How does photosynthesis affect the food we eat?" Students were encouraged to think critically about how plants provide energy for crops and animals, fostering connections between the scientific concept and real-world applications. Building on this discussion, advanced students were tasked with writing a short paragraph explaining how photosynthesis supports ecosystems, pushing them to use their vocabulary in a more analytical way.

To tie everything together, students created mini-posters illustrating the steps of photosynthesis. Each poster included a labeled diagram and descriptive sentences, such as "Sunlight hits the leaves" or "The plant releases oxygen." These projects combined creativity with academic content, providing students with an engaging way to demonstrate their understanding. For added engagement, students participated in a gallery walk, presenting their posters to classmates and answering questions. This not only reinforced their knowledge but also allowed them to practice speaking skills in an academic setting.

Throughout the lesson, we assessed student understanding using a variety of methods. During discussions, we observed which students actively participated and how effectively they used new vocabulary in their responses. For example, students demonstrated their understanding when answering questions like "Why do plants need water?" Additionally, we reviewed the accuracy of their completed sentence strips and evaluated the clarity of their mini-posters. When students presented their posters to the class, we noted how well they could explain the photosynthesis process using academic language. These assessments provided insight into each student's progress in listening, speaking, reading, and writing, while identifying areas where additional support might be needed.

Reflecting on this collaborative lesson, I saw how the integration of visuals, targeted language practice, and teacher collaboration created an inclusive and effective learning environment. The combination of structured activities and creative expression helped students connect challenging vocabulary to scientific concepts, understand the significance of photosynthesis, and apply their knowledge in meaningful ways. Watching them share ideas and build confidence reminded me of the power of blending content knowledge with language development to support English learners in the classroom.

Teacher Tip

Art doesn't need to be reserved for special projects; it can easily become part of your everyday teaching toolkit. Whether it's a powerful painting, a funny cartoon, or a simple photo, visuals have a way of stopping students in their tracks and drawing them in. In fact, images capture everyone's attention, including ours as teachers.

You can start small: show a photo and ask, "What do you see?" Then follow up with, "What else do you see?" These simple questions often lead to rich, unexpected discussions. Use the image to practice adjectives, introduce new vocabulary, or review action verbs. Over time, you can connect visuals to deeper topics, like cultural identity, historical events, or even scientific processes such as photosynthesis.

Choose images that feel real and relevant to your students, ones that reflect their backgrounds, experiences, or interests. Keep a folder of visuals nearby so you can grab one whenever a lesson needs a little energy. And don't stress about making it perfect. What matters most is that students are engaged, thinking, and using language to make sense of the world around them.

Parent Tip

You don't need to be a teacher or an artist to help your child learn through visuals. Some of the best learning happens in the simplest moments. A family photo, a piece of art on the wall, a picture in a magazine, or even an ad on a bus, any of these can spark meaningful language practice. Next time you're flipping through a photo album or scrolling together, pause and explore an image side by side. Ask gentle, open-ended questions like "What do you see?" or "What do you think is happening here?" You might be surprised by what your child notices.

If they point to something, help build on It naturally: if they say "tree," you might respond, "Yes, a tall green tree. Look how big it is!" These everyday conversations, even if they're just a few words, help your child feel more confident using English. You're not just building vocabulary; you're making language part of your shared experience. And the best part? It doesn't feel like homework, it just feels like quality time together.

9 Crafting Personal Narratives Through Visual Inspiration

Teaching personal narrative writing to English learners, especially newcomers, can seem overwhelming at first. Language barriers often make it difficult for students to organize their thoughts and express themselves fully. Using images as a foundation, however, provides a clear and creative way to help students break down the process into manageable steps, starting with narrowing their topics and expanding their ideas. This approach not only supports newcomers but also motivates all students, encouraging them to share meaningful stories with confidence and pride. It's also important to recognize that students who have a strong writing foundation in their first language (L1) can often transfer those skills to English (L2) once they have acquired enough vocabulary and sentence structure.

Narrow the Topic

This lesson begins with the concept of narrowing a topic, which helps students focus on one small, meaningful moment rather than trying to write about everything.

To explain how to narrow the topic, I used hand motions, spreading my arms wide to represent a large, overwhelming topic and then bringing them closer together to show how narrowing the focus makes writing easier. I modeled this idea with an example: "I went to Dallas with my friend Heddy. We visited a teachers' meeting and got lost on the way there." Instead of writing about the whole trip, I explained that I could narrow my topic to just one moment, getting lost on the way to the meeting.

To make this concept more visual, I displayed a photo of a child holding a trophy. I asked the class, "What can you tell me about this moment? Why is it special?" By focusing on the child's proud expression and the context of the photo, we practiced narrowing the topic to one small, impactful moment. Students then brainstormed their own ideas using their personal photos or drawings. For newcomers, I provided sentence frames like:

- "This is a photo of ___."
- "In this picture, I am ___."

One of my students, Linh, used this technique to create a project titled "A Day in My Life." She selected simple photos of her daily routine, such as eating breakfast with her family, walking to school, and playing soccer in the park. At first, her captions were straightforward: "This is my brother. We play soccer." With encouragement, she expanded her sentences: "My brother and I play soccer in the park every day. He is very good at kicking the ball." Her willingness to share her project inspired her classmates, creating an encouraging atmosphere where all students felt empowered to tell their stories.

Expand One Idea

Once students had narrowed their topics, the next step was to expand their ideas by adding meaningful details.

I explained that expanding an idea is like blowing up a balloon. "When we write, we take a small idea and make it bigger," I told the class as I mimed inflating a balloon.

To illustrate this, I returned to my Dallas example:

- Who? My friend Heddy and I.
- What? We got lost on the way to a teachers' meeting.
- Where? On a busy highway.
- When? Early in the morning.
- How? We didn't have a map.
- Why? We were rushing and missed the exit.

Students practiced this expansion technique with their own topics, focusing on adding layers of detail to their writing. For example, Linh chose to expand her story about playing soccer with her brother. Guided by targeted questions such as "Where do you play? Who is there? Why is it special?" she began to transform her initial sentence into a vivid narrative. Linh explained that she and her brother often played on an empty school field near their home, describing the cracked pavement, the faded goalposts, and the distant sound of birds chirping. She added that their games were sometimes joined by neighborhood friends, creating a lively and competitive atmosphere. When prompted to reflect on why this experience was special, Linh revealed that these games were her favorite moments to bond with her brother, who was usually busy with schoolwork. By answering these questions, Linh was able to develop richer, more engaging sentences that painted a vivid picture for her audience. This technique not only improved her storytelling but also gave her the confidence to expand on her ideas and make personal connections to her writing. Through this process, students learned how asking and answering thoughtful questions could transform a simple story into a compelling narrative.

Sharing and Celebrating Stories

Linh's project, "A Day in My Life," beautifully showed how images can unlock a student's voice. When I later shared her work at a professional development workshop for teachers, I held up her timeline with pride. As I walked them through her journey, from basic captions to a rich, personal narrative, I could see the room begin to understand what I had witnessed firsthand: how a quiet newcomer could blossom into a confident storyteller when given the right tools.

That moment reminded me why I believe so deeply in visual storytelling. It isn't just about making writing more engaging, it's about giving students, especially English learners, a way to express parts of themselves they may not yet have the words for. Linh's project didn't just show creativity, it reflected courage, growth, and the quiet power of images to draw out what's inside.

I saw that same power at work in Andrés, a seventh grader who had always met writing time with a sigh and the words, "I can't write." He struggled, not with ideas, but with getting them down. So I gave the class a simple, low-stress assignment: bring in a photo of a family member and write a short description. The next day, Andrés came in holding a picture of his younger brother, and for the first time, he couldn't wait to share. His story began:

"This is my younger brother. He is three years old. He is the youngest of all. He runs and plays like he was born in Philadelphia."

It was a small moment, one I will never forget. His smile said it all: I have something to say. And I just said it.

For Andrés, this project marked a breakthrough. The photo provided a focal point, helping him organize his ideas and build sentences with confidence. When he shared his project with the class, the pride in his voice was unmistakable. The image gave him the push he needed to take that first step into writing. The class clapped after he finished because they understood how hard it had been for him to write. This moment was transformative—not just for Andrés, but for everyone in the room. Ever since that moment, I began to notice remarkable improvement in his writing, which in turn impacted his reading skills.

Writing and reading are closely interrelated, with improvement in one domain often leading to measurable gains in the other. As Andrés developed greater confidence in written expression, he began demonstrating increased engagement with academic texts, applying higher-level vocabulary, improved sentence structure, and more effective comprehension strategies. This progress was confirmed by his Grade 8 STAAR reading assessment, where he met the state's proficiency standard, a meaningful indicator of his academic growth.

Andrés's success reinforced the power of using visual aids to inspire growth in both writing and reading. It showed how these two skills build on each other, breaking down barriers for students who might feel overwhelmed by the blank page or a challenging text. His story highlights how an intentional, creative approach can lead to meaningful, lasting progress

For advanced English learners, images spark a different kind of creativity. They invite students not just to write, but to reflect, to relive, and to express what matters most to them. I'll always remember Maria, one of my advanced students, and the project she created called "The Best Day of My Summer" (see Figure 9.1). She chose a photo of herself and her friends running out of the sea at sunset, laughing, carefree, completely in the moment.

Her writing began:

"As the sun went down, I was running with my friends as we left the sea, admiring the peaceful view. At this moment, I felt like life couldn't get any better."

But she didn't stop there. Maria took us into the rest of that evening, an impromptu house party, card games, music, and conversations about life and friendship. Her story ended with a line that stayed with me:

"This summer, I learned that life is all about living to the fullest so we can remember these moments, the moments that made us feel alive, young, and free."

Moments like these remind me why I use visuals in the classroom. Whether it's Andrés, writing his very first paragraph with pride, or Maria, reflecting deeply on a memory that shaped her, images give students something real to hold onto. They help students find their voice, not just in English, but in who they are and what they have to say.

Finally, this chapter emphasizes project-based learning and visual storytelling as powerful tools for student engagement and critical thinking. For example, a project like "A Day in My Life" allows students to craft narratives that reflect their own perspectives. Through this process, students learn to structure a story, make deliberate choices about what they want to communicate, and develop empathy as they explore the stories of others.

Watching students transform their personal experiences into polished visual stories is one of the most rewarding aspects of teaching with photography.

Building on this foundation, I used to guide students in creating digital stories with a program called PhotoStory. It was a powerful tool in its time, students could combine photos, text, and voice to tell their stories. But since it's no longer supported, I've shifted to using more current, student-friendly platforms like Adobe Express, Canva, and even AI-based tools that let students generate images or record voiceovers with ease.

BEST DAY OF MY SUMMER

Maria Riiginiadi

As the sun goes down ,I was running with my friend as we're getting out of the sea , admiring the peaceful view, and at this moment I felt like life couldn't get any better.

■ This was one of the best days of the summer, the kind of day that makes you feel like life is good and it's worth living. This day was a normal day in which my friends and I have decided to do something different

Figure 9.1 Maria's photos capture the exact moment that inspired her reflective narrative, running out of the sea at sunset, surrounded by friends, and realizing that life, in that fleeting instant, felt perfect. © Maria Boghdadi used with permission.

The first time we used these newer tools, I could see the excitement lighting up my students' faces. One group used Canva to bring their story settings to life, asking AI to generate a misty forest or a bustling street market. Another student, usually shy about speaking in front of the class, proudly recorded her narration in her own voice—and played it back with a big grin. These tools made storytelling feel real, accessible, and deeply personal.

We begin by selecting photos that represent meaningful moments in their narratives, this helps students visually organize their thoughts. Then they add captions or voice recordings, narrating each part of the story in their own words. These voiceovers aren't just about fluency, but they're moments of pride. Students practice their pronunciation, experiment with tone, and build the confidence to share their voices. Some choose music or transitions to reflect the mood of each scene. One student, Nallely, tweaked the timing of her transitions after feedback from classmates, wanting the rhythm to match her story's emotion more closely. Lian, another student, was encouraged by her peers to add more reflective captions, enhancing the emotional depth of her piece.

After presenting their projects, students take time to reflect in writing. I ask them to journal about the process: What did they learn? What would they change? What are they proud of? Their responses often surprise me. Many write about how moved they were by a classmate's story, or how using their own voice made them feel more "heard" in English than ever before. These moments remind me why I teach.

We also spend time analyzing images to build visual literacy, asking questions like "What does this photo want us to feel?" or "Whose story is being told here, and whose is missing?" One photo of a street market sparked a powerful discussion about representation, color, and reality. These conversations teach students to think critically about the images they see every day, and to make intentional choices when telling their own stories.

Witnessing students grow not only as writers but also as thoughtful creators and communicators is one of the most rewarding parts of my work. Whether they're building a scene with AI or recording a voiceover late into the lunch break, their enthusiasm is contagious. And in every project, I see their confidence growing, one image, one voice, one story at a time.

Teacher Tip

One of the best ways to get English learners excited about writing is to let them show their stories before they write them. Start with a simple photo project, something like "A Day in My Life." You'll be surprised how much students open up when they can choose a picture that means something to them. For beginners, offer sentence starters to help them get going. Most importantly, celebrate every effort, no matter how small. Those little wins are what build their confidence and keep them growing.

Parent Tip

You don't need fancy tools to support your child's language learning, just a photo and a little time together. Sit with your child and look through pictures of special moments, like a birthday, a trip to the park, or a family meal. Ask them gentle questions like "What's going on in this picture?" or "Why do you like this memory?" These conversations help your child find the words to express themselves and show them that their stories matter.

10 Taking Personal Narratives to the Next Level

In the previous chapter, we explored how images can inspire students to write personal narratives by helping them narrow their focus and select meaningful moments to write about. This foundational step is critical for building confidence, especially for ELs, who often find writing intimidating. Now, we'll take those initial ideas a step further by teaching students how to craft engaging leads, strengthen their word choice with dynamic verbs, and incorporate creative techniques like figurative language. These advanced skills not only elevate their narratives but also allow students to express themselves with clarity, creativity, and confidence.

When I began my teaching career, I was assigned to a Grade 7 class preparing for the state writing exam. As a new teacher, I found the task overwhelming; the responsibility of teaching writing, especially to ELs, felt immense. Fortunately, the support of the ESL coordinator was invaluable. She provided me with a binder full of strategies for teaching writing, which became a key resource throughout my teaching career. This binder introduced me to a range of approaches, including narrative writing and the 6+1 Traits of Writing, that I would come to rely on across various grade levels and proficiency stages.

The 6+1 Traits—Ideas, Organization, Voice, Word Choice, Sentence Fluency, Conventions, and Presentation—gave me a structured way to approach writing instruction. This framework allowed me to guide students step by step, helping them understand the building blocks of effective writing. For example, by focusing on Ideas first, students learned to develop one main idea per paragraph with supporting details, using past tense for consistency in storytelling. Later, traits like Organization and Sentence Fluency helped them create a logical flow and improve readability, while Voice encouraged them to express themselves authentically.

Getting middle school students, especially ELs to actually enjoy writing always felt like a little victory. Narrative writing became my go-to. Starting with the basics, making sure their sentences made sense! Then slowly layering in things like transition words (which can be surprisingly tricky for them!), adding bits of dialogue that sounded real, and playing around with verbs that had some punch. That's where the magic started to happen. When they realized they could tell their own stories, connect it to their own lives, it wasn't just homework anymore. You could see them start to find their voice, get a little braver with their ideas. Over time, it was amazing to watch their confidence blossom, their stories getting richer and more detailed.

Building on this foundation, one thing I emphasized was how they started their stories. That first sentence, that hook. I remember telling them, "Think of it like trying to get someone to stop and listen to you in a crowded hallway." To show them what I meant, I'd often pull examples right from their own work. Like this one kid, he wrote about his first time at the park and started with, "The sun was shining, and I could hear kids laughing as I walked toward the swings." It's simple, right? But I'd ask the class, "Doesn't that just make you want to know what happens next?" And they'd usually nod, those middle school nods that aren't always enthusiastic, but still count!

Then I'd be brave and share my own attempts, the not-so-great ones included. I remember trying to get them to understand the importance of a good lead by telling them about the time I got totally lost in a market visiting my grandma. My first try? "I got lost in the market and couldn't find my grandmother." Super exciting, right? I'd pause and give them a look. "So," I'd ask, "are you on the edge of your seat?" Cue the eye rolls and headshakes. Exactly! To really drive home that even for me, writing wasn't always polished from the start, I'd even use a visualizer, you know, those interactive whiteboards, to map out my initial, jumbled thoughts and crossed-out words. It helped them see that the thinking and writing process is often messy, full of false starts and revisions. So then I'd try to make it better, adding some of what we'd been talking about: "The crowded market buzzed with voices and the smell of fresh spices. I spun around, my heart pounding, as I realized my grandmother was nowhere to be seen." You could see when it started to make sense to them. "See?" I'd say, "Action, a little bit of what it felt like, that pulls you in." To help them keep these ideas fresh and readily accessible as they worked on their own stories, I created a poster titled "Types of Strong **Leads**" (see Figure 10.1) and displayed it prominently in the classroom. The poster featured categories such as:

- **Character**: Introducing a character to hook the reader.
- **Setting**: Describing the place or atmosphere to draw readers into the scene.
- **Dialogue**: Starting with a conversation to immediately bring the story to life.
- **Onomatopoeia**: Using sound words like "Crash!" or "Bang!" to grab attention and create energy.

Each type of lead on the poster was paired with a picture to help students visualize the concept. For example, under "Setting," there was an image of a forest, and under "Onomatopoeia," a picture of fireworks bursting in the sky. These visuals reinforced the purpose of each lead and helped students choose the best opening for their own stories. This poster became a living document, and I challenged my students to be active readers, and keep adding leads they encountered in their own books till the end of the school year.

To make the activity interactive, I asked students to bring any book they liked, in any language, and examine the opening sentences. Together, we identified the type of lead the author used and added these examples to the poster. Students were excited to contribute, and soon our list of strong leads grew.

"Now that we've seen how professional writers create engaging leads, let's try writing some of our own," I told the class. I asked them to revisit a personal narrative they had already written and think about how they could rewrite the opening sentence to make it more engaging. "You can use action, dialogue, or even a question," I suggested.

One student, Carlos, rewrote the lead to his story about learning to ride a bike. His original sentence was: "I learned to ride my bike last summer." After some encouragement, he changed it to:

"The handlebars wobbled in my hands as I pedaled down the driveway, my heart racing."

"Much better!" I told him. "This makes the reader feel like they're right there with you."

Figure 10.1 Classroom poster illustrating four types of story leads—Character, Setting, Dialogue, and Onomatopoeia—each paired with a simple visual to help students internalize and apply narrative writing techniques. © Created by Nesreen El-Baz.

We dedicated two to three weeks to this process, giving students ample time to explore, practice, and refine their leads. During this period, we revisited the poster, analyzed more examples, and allowed students to rewrite their leads multiple times. The extended time frame ensured that every student, regardless of their proficiency level, had the opportunity to experiment and develop their skills.

At the end of the lesson sequence, we gathered in a circle to share our revised leads. Each student read their new lead aloud, and the class gave feedback, focusing on how well the lead hooked their attention. Carlos beamed as his classmates praised his description of learning to ride a bike.

"Remember," I told the class, "good writers don't always get their leads right on the first try. It's okay to experiment and rewrite until you find the one that feels just right."

By the end of the unit, the students understood that a strong lead sets the tone for the entire narrative. They left class with their new leads, a growing list of strategies, and a sense of excitement about continuing their stories. With their leads in place, the next step was to strengthen the heart of their narratives by focusing on the words that brought their stories to life: verbs.

Strong verbs are the engines of vivid storytelling, helping readers visualize actions and emotions with clarity and energy. To build on the momentum from the leads unit, I introduced the concept of using strong verbs to replace weaker, more generic ones. Just as their leads had grabbed attention, their verbs would now add movement and color to their stories, making their narratives more dynamic and engaging.

When I introduced my students to the concept of using strong verbs, I wanted them to understand that these verbs do more than describe an action, they bring it to life.

I began the lesson by explaining why strong verbs matter. "When writers use strong verbs, they help readers imagine exactly what is happening," I told the class. To illustrate, I wrote a simple sentence on the board:

"The boy went to the park."

"Does the word 'went' give you a clear picture of how the boy moved to the park?" I asked. The students shook their heads. "Exactly! It doesn't tell us if he ran, strolled, or skipped. Let's make this sentence better by choosing a stronger verb that shows how he moved."

To make the activity fun, I provided the class with a list of strong verbs to replace "went." Words like "crawled," "pranced," "trudged," and "rolled" were included on the list. "Let's see which one fits best," I said. As the students read through the options, they acted them out, turning the lesson into an energetic and memorable experience. One student suggested "skipped," and the class began skipping in place, giggling as they visualized the boy skipping to the park.

"Do you see how the verb changes the entire picture in your head?" I asked, and the students nodded enthusiastically.

Also, to help students move beyond the overused verb "said," we created a "Said Is Dead" chart together as a class. Students brainstormed vivid alternatives for expressing speech, and we wrote their suggestions on color-coded sticky notes. These were displayed on the classroom wall as an easy reference (see Figure 7), featuring expressive dialogue tags like "whispered," "yelled," and "announced." This chart soon became a favorite writing tool. During dialogue writing lessons, students used sentence strips to compose or revise lines of dialogue, deliberately replacing "said" with stronger verbs from the chart. This hands-on approach made their writing more dynamic and helped them internalize the use of expressive verbs in narrative contexts.

The next step was to help students recognize strong verbs in the books they loved. "Today, we're going to be word detectives," I announced with a grin. I handed out short books and poems to small groups and asked them to listen carefully for vivid action words as I read aloud. Each time they spotted a strong verb, they popped up from their seats like toast from a toaster, a move that quickly turned the room into a lively (and slightly chaotic) sea of bouncing heads. They giggled and were clearly amused as they jumped up for words like leaped, shivered, and tiptoed.

Now it was their turn. I handed out slips of paper containing sentences with weak verbs and asked the students to rewrite them using more vivid alternatives. For example, a sentence like "The girl said hello to her friend" became "The girl waved hello to her friend" or "The girl shouted hello to her friend," depending on the context.

Over the next two weeks, we continued practicing with strong verbs. Students regularly added to our class-created Strong Verb chart, building a shared bank of vivid action words. As we worked on their personal narratives, I could see their writing come alive—each sentence painted with the clarity and energy that strong verbs provide.

Once students became more confident in using strong verbs, we turned our attention to how these could elevate their dialogue writing. I introduced the concept of **dialogue** by explaining how it brings stories to life through characters' voices. "Dialogue," I told them, "lets your readers hear your characters speak. It makes your story more real and exciting."

We began by acting as dialogue detectives. I handed out short story excerpts filled with dialogue and said, "We're on a mission to spot the talking parts!" Students identified lines of dialogue and focused on punctuation clues— quotation marks, commas, and periods. "Remember," I said, "dialogue always starts and ends with quotation marks. Look closely for those clues!"

To help them internalize these rules, I modeled writing a dialogue sentence:

Grandma said, "Come inside before the rain starts."

We read it aloud together, emphasizing the pauses created by the punctuation. I then asked, "What happens if I leave out the quotation marks? Does it still sound like someone is talking?" They quickly saw how punctuation creates clarity.

To reinforce the concept, we used sentence strips containing unpunctuated lines of dialogue, such as:

- "I'll huff and I'll puff and I'll blow your house down," said the wolf.
- The princess asked, "Can I try on the glass slipper?"

Working in pairs, students added the missing quotation marks, commas, and speaker attributions. They discussed their choices and shared their answers with the class. The activity was both fun and rewarding, and their confidence grew.

Students began using the chart as a reference during revision, replacing basic tags with more vivid ones that brought their characters' voices to life. To support this, we created a "Said Is Dead" chart (see figure 10.2), filled with student-generated alternatives like whispered, yelled, declared, and responded. Each word was written on a color-coded sticky note and proudly displayed in our classroom. The chart quickly became a favorite resource during writing time, helping students bring clarity, tone, and emotion into their dialogue.

The "Said Is Dead" chart became a favorite reference, and I soon saw students naturally using these expressive verbs into their own writing. Finally, students applied their learning to their own stories. I challenged them to add dialogue to a scene they had already written. "Think about how your

Figure 10.2 "Said Is Dead" classroom poster featuring student-generated alternatives to the overused verb "said," encouraging the use of more vivid, expressive dialogue tags in writing. © Created by Nesreen El-Baz.

characters speak," I said. "What would they say to each other? How would they say it?" One student, Tiffany, shared her revised story about a camping trip with her family:

"Did you hear that noise?" whispered Jake, looking around the dark forest.

"I think it's just the wind," replied Tiffany, though she didn't sound convinced.

The class loved how Tiffany's dialogue added suspense to her story, and her confidence soared after receiving their praise.

By the end of the lesson, students understood how dialogue enriches their narratives by showing, not telling. Over the next week, we continued revising and sharing our work, with these conversations bringing new energy to their writing and helping them see their characters as living, breathing individuals.

Building on this momentum, I shifted the focus to another critical element of storytelling: writing **strong endings**. I began by posing a question to spark their curiosity: "How many of you like reading a story that ends with, 'And then I went home' or 'It was all a dream'?" The students groaned and shook their heads. I nodded and said, "Exactly! Those kinds of endings make you feel like the writer just gave up. A good ending does the opposite—it leaves you with something to think about or feel."

I explained that strong endings can take three different forms. First, a surprise ending leaves the reader amazed or caught off guard. Second, a circle ending connects the final moments back to the beginning of the story, creating a sense of completion. Third, an emotional ending leaves the reader with a strong feeling, whether it's joy, sadness, or inspiration.

We explored examples from books we had read in class. I asked students to flip through their favorite books to identify the type of ending the author had used. Together, we found surprises in mystery stories, like when the villain turned out to be the hero's best friend. We identified circle endings in books that began and ended with the same phrase, such as "I knew this day would change my life forever." And we discovered emotional endings in stories that made us feel proud of the character's journey, like when a protagonist learned the importance of family or courage.

To model how to craft these endings, I revisited a personal story I'd shared earlier about building a treehouse with my cousins. "The first ending I came up with was this: 'And then I went home, and we never tried to build another treehouse.'" I paused, and the students groaned. "Not great, right?" They laughed. "Let's try something better." I showed them three versions:

- **Surprise Ending:** "Just as we finished cleaning up the broken wood, my cousin pulled out a blueprint for a two-story treehouse."
- **Circle Ending:** "Looking at the pile of wood, I remembered how excited we'd been that morning. Maybe, just maybe, we'd try again someday."

- **Feeling Ending:** "Even though the treehouse collapsed, I felt proud of what we had tried to do—and excited about what we could build next."

The students discussed which one they liked best and why. Then, it was their turn to practice.

We repeated the process we used with leads by exploring endings from various books in different genres. The students worked in groups, analyzed the last few sentences of each story, and determined which of the three types of endings the author had used. This activity not only helped them understand the different techniques but also inspired them to think creatively about their own writing.

Next, I asked students to revisit a personal narrative they had already written and brainstorm at least two new endings. For example, Chi-An, who had written about her experience baking cookies with her grandmother, originally ended her story with, "And then we ate the cookies." After exploring the different types of endings, she rewrote hers as a circle ending: "As I bit into the cookie, I remembered what Grandma always said, 'The secret ingredient is love.'" Then she tried an emotional ending: "Looking at Grandma, I realized the cookies weren't the best thing about that day, she was." Both versions captured the warmth and meaning of her story in a way her original ending hadn't.

For about a week, we experimented with writing endings, revising them, and sharing them with peers. By the end of the lesson, the students understood that an ending isn't just about wrapping up the story; it's about leaving the reader with something to think about, feel, or even remember long after they've finished reading. As we wrapped up, I reminded them, "Just like a strong lead pulls your reader in, a strong ending stays with them. So, give it your best shot!"

Once students had a strong grasp of crafting leads and endings, we shifted our focus to the transitions that would hold their stories together. Many of my students struggled with writing that felt disconnected or choppy, so we tackled the power of **transition words** head-on. I explained how transitions serve as bridges, guiding readers smoothly from one idea to the next. To help them understand their purpose, I categorized transition words by their use: sequencing transitions like "first," "next," and "finally"; words for adding information such as "moreover" and "in addition"; contrasting transitions like "however" and "on the other hand"; and cause-and-effect transitions such as "therefore" and "as a result."

Using student work as examples, including Juan's "Alma Story," we explored how replacing simple transitions like "first" and "then" with more advanced options like "initially" or "following that" could make their writing more polished and engaging. Students then revised their own stories, adding stronger transitions in a different pen color, allowing them to see how these changes improved the flow and clarity of their writing. By reflecting on these revisions, they realized how transitions made their stories clearer and more logical, ultimately gaining confidence in their ability to elevate the readability of their work.

By teaching students how to use transitions effectively, I saw their writing transform from a collection of disconnected ideas into cohesive, flowing narratives. Each revision brought clarity and sophistication to their work, as they began to connect their thoughts with purpose.

This focus on transitions not only enhanced their storytelling but also gave them a critical tool for their academic writing, preparing them for more advanced tasks. Confidence grew, their writing became more polished and professional, and their progress was evident to both their peers and me.

The TELPAS and TAKS results from 2009 to 2010 demonstrate how these strategies transformed student outcomes. For instance, students who began the year hesitant to express themselves in writing showed remarkable improvement, not only in their language proficiency ratings but also in their ability to craft compelling narratives. Many moved from intermediate to advanced or advanced-high levels on the TELPAS writing component, reflecting significant growth in their command of the English language.

Similarly, the TAKS writing scores revealed steady progress, with students achieving scores well above the passing threshold. This improvement wasn't limited to one or two high achievers; it was evident across the class, showcasing how project-based learning, visual storytelling, and focused writing instruction can have a broad and transformative impact.

The results were not just numbers on a spreadsheet, they represented the growth of students who entered the classroom unsure of their abilities and left as confident writers. These scores were a testament to their hard work and the power of creative, student-centered teaching. By combining innovative strategies with clear expectations, students were able to express themselves authentically, meet academic benchmarks, and, most importantly, discover joy and pride in their writing. The Table 10.1 offers a snapshot of this growth across the cohort.

Table 10.1 Student performance on TELPAS and TAKS writing exams shows significant growth. Data is anonymized and drawn from real student outcomes. All identifying information has been removed to ensure confidentiality.

Student ID number	Student's Name	ELA TAKS Reading 08/09	ELA TAKS Reading Score 09/10	Grade	TELPAS 2009 Comp Rating	TELPAS 2010 Comp Rating	TELPAS 2009 Writing	TELPAS 2010 Writing	TAKS Writing Score 09/10
	Student 1			7		A		Int	
	Student 2			7		A		Int	
	Student 3			7		AH		A	
	Student 4		536	7	A	Int	Int	AH	1943
	Student 5		561	7	Int	Int	AH	AH	2010
	Student 6		508	7	B	Int	Int	A	1978
	Student 7		741	7	AH	AH	A	AH	2230
	Student 8		614	7	AH	AH	A	AH	2212
	Student 9		683	7	A	AH	A	AH	2102
	Student 10		701	7	A	AH	Int	AH	2147
	Student 11		636	7	A	A		AH	2249
	Student 12		584	7	B	A		AH	2100

Student ID number	Student's Name	ELA TAKS Reading 08/09	ELA TAKS Reading Score 09/10	Grade	TELPAS 2009 Comp Rating	TELPAS 2010 Comp Rating	TELPAS 2009 Writing	TELPAS 2010 Writing	TAKS Writing Score 09/10
	Student 13		614	7	AH	AH	A	AH	2364
	Student 14		683	7	A	A	AH	AH	2179
	Student 15		599	7	A	A	Int	AH	2117
	Student 16		659	7	A	AH	AH	AH	2249
	Student 17		508	7					1906
	Student 18		659	7	A	A	Int	AH	2147
	Student 19		614	7	A	A	Int	A	2056
	Student 20		636	7	AH	AH	A	AH	2179
	Student 21		621	7		AH		AH	1925
	Student 22			7		Int		B	
	Student 23		753	7					
	Student 24		659	7	AH	AH	AH	AH	2268

Teacher Tip

When teaching writing techniques like leads, strong verbs, and endings, give students plenty of time to experiment and revise their work. Use anchor charts or posters as visual aids and integrate real-world examples from literature to inspire students. Allow them to practice in collaborative settings, like peer reviews or group discussions, to build their confidence. Celebrate their progress by having a class showcase where they share their favorite leads, most vivid verbs, or most creative endings. This not only validates their hard work but also reinforces the sense that writing is a skill that grows with practice.

Parent Tip

Encourage your child to share their writing projects at home. Ask them to read their favorite sentences aloud, and praise their creativity and effort. You can also support their learning by reading books together and pointing out engaging leads, strong action words, or meaningful endings. Highlight how professional authors use these techniques, and ask your child how they might use similar strategies in their own stories. This makes writing a shared and enjoyable experience while building their confidence and enthusiasm for storytelling.

11 Descriptive Writing: Connecting Language to Life

Descriptive writing is more than just a language skill, it's a powerful gateway for ELs to express themselves and connect with their own stories. When students describe objects that hold personal meaning, they're not just learning new words or practicing grammar; they're exploring their identities and finding their voices as writers. It's in these moments, when they write about something that truly matters to them, that writing becomes authentic. It becomes a way to say, "This is who I am."

One of the most impactful ways to nurture this kind of writing is by using real-life objects from students' own lives. A beloved bicycle, a backpack covered in signatures, a treasured toy, these aren't just things; they're memory holders. They spark emotions, memories, and rich language. By describing the color, shape, texture, and even the sound or smell of these items, students are guided naturally into using sensory details. And when they share objects that reflect their cultural backgrounds, the classroom transforms into a space of shared stories, curiosity, and deep respect.

This lesson plan offers a step-by-step approach to help students craft their own descriptive pieces, starting with a simple, yet meaningful object, a vintage music box. Together, the class explores its features: the smooth, polished wood, the intricate carvings, the soft, tinkling sound. Words like antique, delicate, and ornate are introduced to enrich their descriptions. Then, students read a model essay about the music box, breaking it down as a group—What did the writer describe first? How did they use sensory language? Why is the object special to them?

Through this process, students not only learn how to structure their own writing, but they also begin to understand the deeper value of their own experiences. They see that their voices matter, their stories have weight, and their words can touch others. In the end, it's not just about writing a paragraph, it's about discovering the storyteller within.

Students then move into guided writing, selecting their own personal objects and creating outlines based on the model essay. They describe the object's appearance, share its history or significance, and reflect on its emotional meaning. Examples of student writing are shared to inspire creativity and illustrate the impact of sensory details. For example, Nour wrote about his signed backpack (see Figure 11.1):

"My backpack may not be fancy, but it holds memories. Every time I wear it, I remember meeting Xavi Hernandez and the excitement of getting his signature. It's not just a bag, it's a piece of my life's story."

A second descriptive essay focuses on a treasured Parker pen inherited from the student's grandfather (see Figure 11.2), an object rich with historical and emotional resonance. Through poetic imagery and cultural references, the student transforms a simple pen into a symbol of memory, legacy, and imagination.

These examples demonstrate how personal meaning and sensory detail can elevate even the simplest objects into compelling narratives. One student reflected, "I didn't realize how much better my writing had gotten until I looked back." This reflective practice not only built their confidence, but also motivated them to keep pushing forward—seeing tangible growth made the effort feel worthwhile.

At the end of each major writing unit, students chose one piece from their portfolio to revise in depth. They applied skills they had developed throughout the year, enhancing imagery, refining transitions, and sharpening their voice, to strengthen and elevate their work. This process of revisiting and reshaping their writing emphasized that effective writing is not about perfection on the first try, but about revision, persistence, and growth.

Portfolios became more than just a tool for tracking progress; they evolved into a celebration of each student's voice, creativity, and personal journey.

A signed backpack

My very special object which I am going to talk about is a very unique backpack signed by XAXI HERNANDEZ , one of the best football players and midfielders of all time . it was a gift from my mother , it's a blue and black rubber backpack that contains two zippers . it is not unique for its style or form , actually it's not very beautiful and elegant. But the story and the memories that this backpack brings are the reason it's special for me. It is located in the top shelf of my wardrobe beside my shoes that is also signed by the same player . Everyone is allowed to see it and I like when people see it because they keep talking about how lucky I am to have a gift like that and we talk about Xavi and how he was a great player . every time I wear it I remember the days in the camp with one of my favorite players when he came to Egypt and how I fought and suffered to get that signature between dozens of kids . Also the backpack reminds me of the days when Xavi was a Barcelona player before he left the club. So that nostalgia moment that it brings me is what makes it very unique and special backpack.

Figure 11.1 Nour's descriptive essay about a treasured backpack signed by football legend Xavi Hernández illustrates personal achievement, cultural pride, and meaningful memories. This piece has been preserved in its original form to highlight his authentic voice and identity through sport. © Nour Amr used with permission.

By year's end, students viewed their collections with pride, recognizing not only how much they had improved as writers, but how they had learned to express themselves in vivid, meaningful ways. For both teacher and student, the portfolio stood as a powerful testament to what writing can do: nurture confidence, deepen thinking, and foster transformation.

My Parker Pen

On my writing table, between my French dictionary and my music box, there is a luxury Parker pen without which I feel that I couldn't write. It's actually my favorite pen and the best pen I've ever used. I've received it from my grandfather 4 years ago.

No one beside me can see the magic and the calligraphy that it does. Without it, I couldn't think. In my notebook, there are blue rivers that came from this pen.

This gold pen shines in the light of the sun with great brightness. On the side of the pen lies my grandfather's name. Engraved on the side, it says M. Kamel. The ink that comes out of the pen is the color of the water on the beach in Alexandria. This pen was made in the 19th century. It was used by great writers and authors before. It's handmade. It makes me remember the past and I feel that I live in another world, another year, and another century.

It was first used by Mohamed Ali and King Farouk the First. It was also used by Ahmed Chawki. It tells me the past and the history of Egypt and a lot of things that no one knows.

It does a lot of things for me, but eventually, it can't make some stuff. It can't get the full mark in the exam. It can't make friends. When I couldn't find it, it can't say where it is.

Despite the stuff that it can't do, it makes me happy and comforted. It's the friend.

This pen is not for sale. My grandfather gave it to me because he knew that I would be a good writer. He was very happy when he was giving it to me. He also told me that this is the best gift I could ever get.

Figure 11.2 Omar's descriptive essay about a cherished family heirloom, "My Parker Pen," captures the emotional connection to his grandfather, his aspirations as a writer, and cultural ties to Egyptian history. © Omar Ossama used with permission.

Teacher Tip

Invite students to take pride in their writing portfolios by giving them a sense of ownership over how they are presented. Let them decorate their covers with drawings, photos, or meaningful symbols, and encourage them to add a personal "About the Author" page at the beginning. This small touch helps students see their portfolios not just as a collection of assignments but as a reflection of who they are becoming as writers. It makes the process feel more personal and more purposeful. During review sessions, take time to celebrate their progress. Point out specific ways their writing has grown, whether it is richer sensory details, more vivid language, or clearer sentence flow. These moments of recognition help students see just how far they have come and give them the confidence to keep going.

Parent Tip

You can play a meaningful role in your child's writing journey by simply asking them to share their portfolio with you at home. Sit together and explore their favorite pieces, ask what inspired them, what they enjoyed writing about, and what they're most proud of. Celebrate their progress, and invite them to tell you how their writing has changed or improved over time. Even if English isn't your first language, your interest means the world to them. Just by listening and showing curiosity, you're giving your child a powerful message: Your voice matters. These shared moments not only boost their confidence, but also help them feel proud of their growth and more connected to their learning.

12 Interactive Listening and Speaking

Developing strong listening and speaking skills is essential for ELs, as these skills form the foundation for effective communication in both academic and real-world settings. In my classroom, I've discovered that interactive and creative approaches make a significant difference in engaging students and building their confidence. For me, teaching listening and speaking has never just been about preparing for exams; it's about equipping students with the tools to navigate the world beyond the classroom.

One year, I introduced CNN Student News (now CNN 10) to my students as a way to practice listening skills while staying informed about current events. The excitement in the classroom was palpable as they listened to engaging news segments designed for students, sparking lively discussions about the stories they heard. What made this activity especially impactful was the built-in resources provided by CNN, such as ready-made questions and a script of the news segments. Printing the transcripts allowed students to follow along, improving their listening comprehension and giving them a reference for unfamiliar vocabulary or phrases. After viewing, students would work in pairs or groups to discuss the topics, creating their own questions and answering them collaboratively. This added layer of interaction not only reinforced the content but also encouraged critical thinking and the use of English in authentic, meaningful ways. Over time, students began to express their own perspectives more confidently, discussing global issues and even drawing connections to their own lives. Moments like these remind me of the importance of balancing skill development with engaging activities that connect students to the world beyond the classroom.

Role play has also been a transformative tool in helping students develop their speaking skills, especially for ELs. Stepping into a role offers a sense of liberation; students often feel less self-conscious and more willing to take risks with their language because it's the "character" speaking, not them. One memorable activity involved a restaurant scenario where students practiced ordering food. With printed menus and scripted dialogue as a starting point, they gradually transitioned into improvisation, learning to adjust to dynamic exchanges while sharing plenty of laughter. This activity not only reduced their anxiety but also connected language learning to practical, real-life situations. To keep role play fresh and challenging, I expanded the scenarios to include doctor's appointments, job interviews, and even group problem-solving tasks, rotating roles to give students diverse opportunities to practice different aspects of communication. Additionally, I encouraged students to take part in drama classes, where acting out scenes from novels or other texts allowed them to develop their language skills in a fun, immersive environment. These experiences helped students build confidence, fluency, and creativity while fostering teamwork and empathy. To deepen the learning process, I incorporated self-assessment and peer feedback, which encouraged students to reflect on their progress and identify areas for improvement. Role play became not just an exercise in speaking but a gateway to deeper engagement with language and culture.

Incorporating music into lessons has been another game-changer for engaging students and enhancing language acquisition. Songs have a unique way of bringing energy and joy into the classroom while serving as a powerful resource for teaching rhythm, intonation, pronunciation, and vocabulary. One day, I invited students to bring in their favorite songs to share with the class. Some chose popular English tracks, while others introduced songs from their native languages, offering heartfelt explanations of the lyrics in English. This simple activity blossomed into a beautiful cultural exchange, where students felt pride in sharing a piece of their identity while honing their language skills. Together, we analyzed song lyrics, identifying new vocabulary, idiomatic expressions, and cultural references. Breaking down the structure of the songs allowed students to see how language is used creatively, while also reinforcing grammar and syntax in a memorable context.

To take it a step further, I incorporated songs with repetitive structures and simple lyrics, such as children's songs or pop hits, to help students internalize sentence patterns and vocabulary. These songs made lessons not only effective but also enjoyable, as students found themselves humming or singing phrases long after the lesson ended. For example, songs with clear choruses became excellent tools for practicing stress and intonation, while upbeat tracks energized even the shyest learners to participate. Occasionally, we wrote our own lyrics to familiar melodies, turning songwriting into a creative exercise that connected language to personal expression. In one lesson, students composed group verses describing their daily routines, using targeted vocabulary and grammar. These activities demonstrated how music not only reinforces language skills but also creates a supportive, inclusive classroom atmosphere. Whether analyzing complex lyrics or singing simple tunes, music has consistently proven to be a medium that transcends linguistic barriers, making lessons engaging, culturally rich, and unforgettable.

In addition to role play and music, I often use activities that directly target listening and speaking skills. For instance, playing short audio clips and asking students to summarize or respond encourages active listening. Another favorite is predictive listening, before playing an audio clip, I ask students to guess its content based on a title or an image, then compare their predictions to the actual material. These strategies keep students engaged while improving their comprehension and critical thinking.

Interactive approaches to listening and speaking provide more than just language practice—they create a supportive and dynamic environment where students feel confident to take risks and grow. By blending creativity with purpose, we not only teach language but also inspire students to become effective communicators in all aspects of their lives.

To further enhance students' listening and speaking skills, structured activities and targeted tools are invaluable. Providing sentence stems is one effective way to scaffold speaking tasks and encourage meaningful conversations. For example, when students are working in pairs or small groups, sentence-stems like "I agree with ___ because … " or "One way to solve this problem is … "give them a framework to articulate their thoughts. These guided conversations build confidence by allowing students to focus on their ideas without the added pressure of figuring out how to phrase them. Another approach I've used is peer summaries, where one student shares an idea, and their partner listens attentively before repeating or summarizing what they heard. This activity not only strengthens listening skills but also encourages students to engage deeply with one another's perspectives.

Group discussions and presentations offer another dynamic avenue for practicing these skills. Discussion circles, where each student takes on a specific role such as discussion leader or note-taker, ensure that everyone is actively participating. By rotating roles, students develop a range of skills, from leading conversations to actively listening and synthesizing information. To reduce anxiety, I encourage students to practice presentations with a partner or small group before sharing with the whole class. This layered approach provides a safe space for practice while gradually building their confidence for more public speaking.

Podcasts and audio diaries are modern, creative ways to engage students in speaking practice, offering them opportunities to explore their voices and interests in a meaningful context. I've seen the excitement in students when they create their own podcasts on topics they're passionate about, from their favorite hobbies to cultural traditions or even current events. The process of brainstorming ideas, scripting their episodes, recording, and sharing their work with peers transforms speaking practice into a dynamic, authentic experience. Not only do students develop fluency and confidence as they articulate their thoughts, but they also learn important skills such as organizing their ideas, adjusting tone for their audience, and using technology effectively. Group podcasts add another layer of collaboration, requiring students to negotiate roles, interact spontaneously, and practice conversational English as they produce something creative together.

Audio diaries, on the other hand, provide a more personal and reflective way to develop speaking skills. Students can record their daily thoughts, reflections on lessons, or even reactions to articles and videos, turning speaking practice into a habit. Over time, listening to their recordings allows them to track their progress, noticing improvements in fluency, pronunciation, and clarity. For instance, one student who struggled with verb tense use began to catch and correct these errors after hearing herself speak during diary reviews. These moments of self-awareness are transformative, encouraging students to take ownership of their learning journey.

To enhance these activities further, I often incorporate peer feedback, where students listen to each other's podcasts or diary entries and provide constructive comments. This fosters a sense of community and collaboration while helping students learn from one another. Occasionally, I extend the activities into classroom projects, such as creating a podcast series on a shared theme or turning individual audio diaries into oral storytelling assignments.

These projects not only build language skills but also empower students to share their unique perspectives, making speaking practice both personal and impactful.

By integrating modern tools like podcasts and audio diaries, I've found that students not only improve their communication skills but also gain confidence, creativity, and a deeper connection to the learning process.

Listening for gist and detail is another key skill I emphasize in class. Gist listening involves asking students to listen to an audio clip and summarize the main idea, helping them focus on understanding the overall message. On a second listen, they can shift their attention to specific details, such as key facts or names, sharpening their ability to concentrate on information. This dual approach mirrors the way we process information in real-world situations, making it both practical and engaging for students.

Technology also plays an important role in supporting listening and speaking practice. Language-learning apps like Duolingo or BBC Learning English offer interactive, self-paced opportunities for students to build their skills outside of the classroom. Platforms like VoiceThread or Flipgrid encourage students to participate in online discussions, where they can record their responses in a low-pressure environment. These tools not only extend learning beyond the classroom but also cater to a variety of learning styles, making practice more accessible and enjoyable for all students.

By incorporating these varied activities, guided conversations, group discussions, podcasts, technology-based tools, and structured listening exercises, teachers can create an engaging and supportive environment that empowers students to grow into confident communicators. These strategies do more than just teach language; they build skills that students will carry with them into their academic journeys and beyond, equipping them to thrive in an interconnected world.

Teacher Tip

Mix and match these strategies to keep your lessons fresh, dynamic, and engaging. Whether you're using role play, music, podcasts, or any other interactive approach, the key is to create authentic contexts where students can practice language in meaningful ways. Role play helps them navigate real-world scenarios, music brings energy and rhythm to language learning, and podcasts allow them to explore their passions while building fluency and confidence. By combining these techniques, you can cater to diverse learning styles and interests, ensuring every student finds an activity that resonates with them. It's also essential to foster an environment where students feel safe to experiment with language and make mistakes.

Celebrate their progress, encourage collaboration, and incorporate activities that challenge them to stretch their skills without feeling overwhelmed. When students are actively engaged and see the relevance of what they're learning to their own lives, their motivation soars, and their confidence grows. Ultimately, these strategies aren't just about language practice—they're about empowering students to find their voice and take ownership of their learning journey. With creativity and intentional planning, you can create lessons that are not only effective but also memorable and transformative for your students.

Parent Tip

Encourage your child to explore English through songs, audiobooks, or podcasts at home. These resources not only make language learning enjoyable but also provide valuable exposure to authentic pronunciation, rhythm, and vocabulary. For example, after listening to a song or story, ask your child to explain its meaning or summarize it in their own words. This reinforces their listening skills while boosting their ability to process and articulate ideas in English. For younger learners, you can turn it into a game by having them act out parts of the story or guess the meanings of key phrases. Older children can delve deeper, analyzing lyrics or discussing the themes and messages of a podcast episode. Joining in on these activities can also be a wonderful way to bond as a family while supporting your child's language development. Singing songs together, discussing favorite audiobooks, or even starting a family podcast club where each member shares their thoughts can make English practice a shared, enjoyable experience. Encouraging regular engagement with these resources helps create a relaxed and supportive environment, where your child feels motivated and confident to use English beyond the classroom. Over time, these habits will not only improve their listening and speaking skills but also instill a lifelong love of learning.

13 Using Picture Books and Read-alouds to Enhance Language Learning

Picture books are powerful tools in language instruction, offering a range of benefits that significantly enhance learners' linguistic and cognitive development. They are particularly effective in enriching vocabulary, as the language in picture books often contains a more diverse array of words compared to everyday conversations.

Research highlights that picture books expose learners to unique word types and more advanced language structures, providing a rich linguistic resource that surpasses child-directed speech. This exposure builds learners' vocabulary and helps them encounter words in meaningful contexts, aiding retention and practical application.

Engaging with picture books also develops learners' narrative skills. Through the natural flow of storytelling, students gain an understanding of story structures, sequencing, and character development. These experiences foster narrative competence, which is critical for both oral and written communication. Learners become better equipped to comprehend and construct coherent stories, a foundational skill for language acquisition.

In addition to linguistic benefits, picture books enhance visual literacy. The interplay of text and illustrations invites learners to interpret visual information alongside the narrative, strengthening comprehension and critical thinking. This multimodal engagement helps learners decode the connections between text and images, improving their ability to analyze, infer, and make meaning from visual cues.

Picture books also play an essential role in fostering cultural awareness and empathy. By introducing learners to diverse cultures, characters, and perspectives, they serve as windows into different experiences and worldviews. This exposure promotes inclusivity and helps students build social awareness, encouraging them to empathize with others and broaden their understanding of the world. As a result, picture books not only teach language but also cultivate emotional and cultural intelligence.

The engaging nature of picture books further motivates learners, transforming reading into an enjoyable and rewarding activity. The combination of vibrant illustrations and compelling narratives captures their interest, making them eager to read more. This motivation is especially valuable for reluctant readers or ELs who may find traditional texts intimidating. By creating a positive and accessible reading experience, picture books foster a lifelong love for learning and literacy.

For diverse learners, particularly ELs and students with varying proficiency levels, picture books offer accessible content that bridges language gaps. The visual context provided by illustrations supports comprehension, making complex ideas easier to understand and more relatable. This accessibility allows teachers to tailor instruction to meet students' individual needs, ensuring that all learners can engage meaningfully with the material.

In my own classroom, I witnessed firsthand how picture books broke down barriers for newcomers and intermediate learners. Many students initially resisted picture books, perceiving them as "for young kids." To address this, I borrowed books from the library and left them accessible to students during advisory time, encouraging them to explore the stories at their own pace. Over time, I observed students feeling safe enough to pick up these books in the ESL classroom, where they knew they wouldn't be judged. The shared understanding that "everyone was learning" created a nurturing environment that empowered them to embrace reading.

Through deliberate planning and enthusiastic modeling, I turned picture book reading into a shared, joyful activity. I created a reading corner in the classroom, where students sat in a circle as I conducted read-aloud sessions. These sessions began with introducing the book's cover, title, author, illustrator, and any awards, helping students become familiar with literary features. Students were invited to make predictions based on the cover, which I wrote on the board. When I read aloud, I adjusted my voice and tone for dialogues to sustain their interest, modeling expressive reading that encouraged them to emulate. Over time, this approach built their confidence, improved their vocabulary, and fostered a genuine love for stories.

Beyond sparking a love for reading, picture books also became powerful tools for teaching essential comprehension strategies, like making inferences. I wanted to show my students that making inferences wasn't something unfamiliar or daunting—it was a skill they already used in their daily lives. To make this process tangible, I introduced it with a visual representation (see Figure 13.1): an eye to symbolize "what you see" and a brain to represent "what you know." Together, these led to a glowing light bulb, symbolizing the moment when an inference is made.

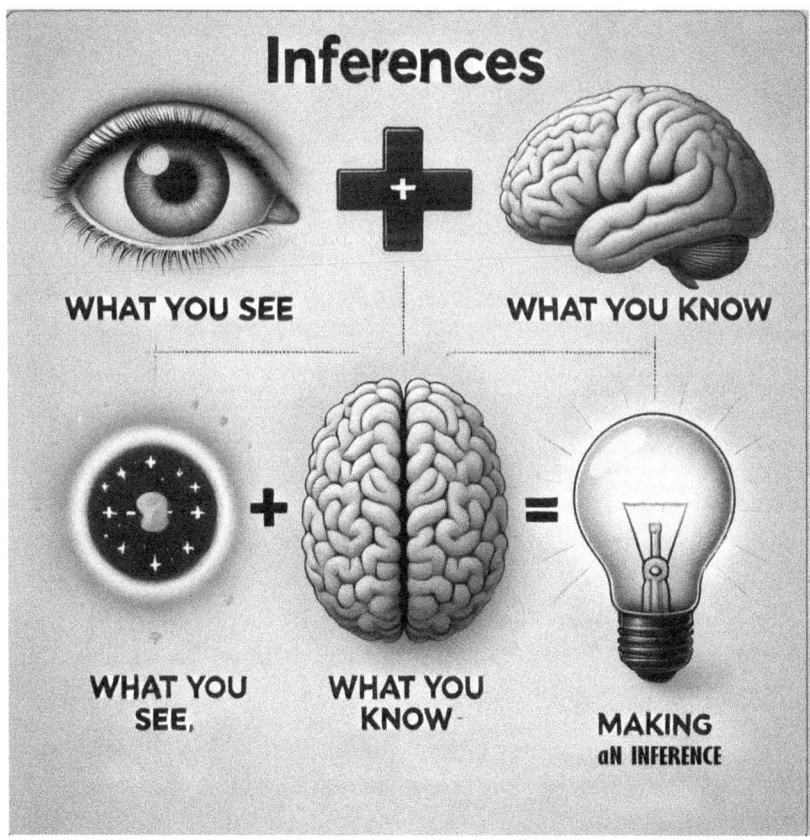

Figure 13.1 A visual aid used to teach inference, illustrating how observations combined with prior knowledge lead to deeper understanding. © Created by Nesreen El-Baz.

I began with a relatable example. "Imagine it's raining outside," I said. "What do you think I might take with me?" When students quickly responded, "An umbrella!" I used their answer to show how they had just made an inference, combining what they observed (the rain) with what they already knew (that umbrellas keep people dry). Their faces lit up as they realized they had been using this skill all along without even knowing its name. This moment became the perfect starting point for teaching inferences through picture books.

Using *Where the Wild Things Are* by Maurice Sendak, I guided my students through the process step by step. We analyzed the book's cover first, listing observations, connecting them to prior knowledge, and drawing conclusions about Max's emotions and intentions. During read-alouds, I paused at key moments to ask guiding questions, prompting students to combine visual and textual clues with their own knowledge to infer what was happening beneath the surface of the story. I constantly referred to the "Inference Poster" I had created, which outlined the process: "What do I see? What do I know? What can I figure out?"

At the end of the lesson, students practiced making inferences on their own using illustrations from other books. It was incredibly rewarding to hear them excitedly discuss their observations and insights, knowing they were building a critical skill they could apply to any story. As one student put it, "I didn't think I was good at reading between the lines, but now I know I can do it!" That moment solidified for me the power of picture books not just as engaging stories, but as dynamic tools for developing deeper comprehension and critical thinking.

By combining the accessibility of picture books with deliberate instructional strategies, I saw my students grow not only as readers but also as thinkers. They began to see books as more than just words and pictures, they were mysteries waiting to be solved, filled with hidden meanings they could uncover by making inferences. In this way, picture books became not only a bridge to language and literacy but also a doorway to deeper understanding and self-confidence.

Picture books hold a unique power to transform the classroom into a space where all learners can thrive. Through their vibrant illustrations and carefully chosen words, they create an accessible and engaging medium that transcends age, language barriers, and academic levels. In my own experience, picture books have been invaluable tools—not only for sparking a love for reading but also for fostering critical skills like making inferences, which are essential for deep comprehension.

Watching my students grow more confident as readers and thinkers reaffirmed for me the profound impact of these seemingly simple stories. Picture books empowered even the most hesitant learners to explore, connect, and express themselves. They taught my students how to look closely, think deeply, and trust their ability to uncover meaning—skills that extend far beyond the classroom.

As educators, we have the opportunity to harness the magic of picture books to create inclusive, dynamic learning environments. By integrating these stories into our instruction and modeling enthusiasm for their richness, we can help students build the skills, confidence, and curiosity they need to succeed. Ultimately, picture books are far more than tools for teaching; they are gateways to imagination, understanding, and joy.

Teacher Tip

When introducing a new picture book, take a moment to preview the story with your students. Begin by exploring the cover, title, and illustrations. Ask open-ended questions like "What do you notice?" or "What do you think this story might be about?" These questions spark curiosity and activate prior knowledge, setting the stage for deeper engagement. Don't hesitate to model your own thinking as you make predictions or inferences.

By showing students how to connect their observations with their knowledge, you'll build their confidence and help them develop this essential skill.

Parent Tip

Picture books aren't just for little ones, they're powerful tools for learners of all ages, especially when it comes to language development. Whether your child is new to English or simply enjoys stories, picture books offer a rich, visual way to build vocabulary, spark imagination, and deepen understanding.

When reading together at home, pause and talk about the illustrations. Ask open-ended questions like, "What do you think is happening in this picture?"

or "Why might the character feel this way?" Encourage your child to connect what they see with what they already know. These conversations help build critical thinking skills and language confidence.

Most importantly, this simple shared activity becomes a special moment between you and your child, one that supports learning and brings you closer through the joy of storytelling.

14 Creative and Hands-on Approaches to Teach Literature

For ELs, literature can often feel like an insurmountable challenge. Complex vocabulary, unfamiliar cultural references, and dense sentence structures can create barriers that discourage students from engaging with texts. However, by incorporating leveled books and carefully selected literature, teachers can bridge the gap and invite all students, regardless of language proficiency, into the world of storytelling.

Leveled books provide accessible entry points into literature while maintaining rich themes and engaging narratives. For example:

- A Christmas Carol can be found in simplified adaptations that retain the core story of Scrooge's redemption.
- For Romeo and Juliet, abridged versions or graphic novel adaptations offer a visual and simplified approach to understanding Shakespeare's timeless tale.

These leveled texts can serve as scaffolding, preparing students to engage with the original works at a later stage. Pairing them with creative, hands-on activities like clay sculpting, visual storyboards, or character design enables ELs to process and express their understanding in ways that transcend language barriers.

By integrating leveled literature into creative approaches, teachers ensure that every student feels included and empowered to explore the world of literature, no matter where they are in their language journey.

When I introduced *Esperanza Rising* to my ELs, I wasn't sure how they would react. Would they connect with Esperanza's journey, her struggles, and her resilience? Would the language be accessible enough for them to truly enjoy the story? I was determined to create an environment where they felt confident and excited to explore this rich, emotional narrative.

To my delight, the students embraced the story with enthusiasm. For many, it was the first time they saw themselves or their families reflected in a book. As we read about Esperanza's journey from privilege to hardship and her eventual triumph over adversity, I saw their eyes light up with recognition. One student pointed out, "This is like my mom when she moved here!" Another chimed in, "Esperanza is brave, but she's scared, too—like me when I started school." These connections made the story come alive in ways I could never have planned.

In one session, we paused to discuss Esperanza's first day picking crops, a moment that marked a significant shift in her character. I asked the students to imagine themselves in her shoes. "What do you think Esperanza was feeling? How do you know?" At first, they hesitated, but then one student observed, "She must feel tired and sad because she's not used to working. It's like when I had to help my dad at his job—it was so hard." Hearing this sparked a cascade of comments, each building on the other. The room buzzed with energy as they shared their insights and connected their own experiences to Esperanza's struggles.

Similarly, when we read *Tuck Everlasting*, the students were captivated by the magic of the Tuck family's immortality. One student shyly asked, "If you could live forever, would you want to?" I turned the question back to the class, and their responses were profound. Some talked about how they would miss their families if they lived forever, while others said they would want more time to explore the world and achieve their dreams.

These conversations went far beyond the words on the page; they delved into themes of love, loss, and the value of life itself.

In addition to inspiring deep discussions, reading these novels also became a springboard for writing practice. To reinforce grammar concepts like the past tense, I asked students to open their books and circle all the verbs in the past tense they could find in a specific chapter. Together, we created a list of these verbs on the board, discussing their meanings and usage in the story. Then, students used these verbs to write short sentences or summaries about what they had read. For example, they wrote sentences like, "Esperanza worked in the fields," or "She learned to be strong." This exercise not only reinforced grammar but also encouraged students to see how authors use language to bring stories to life.

For *Tuck Everlasting*, I used a similar approach by focusing on descriptive writing. We identified vivid adjectives and sensory details in the text, such as "golden sunlight" or "a bubbling spring." After discussing how these phrases created a magical atmosphere, students practiced writing their own descriptive sentences about places they loved or imagined. Some even attempted to write short paragraphs where they described a "magical" setting inspired by the novel. Through these exercises, reading and writing became interconnected, with one skill naturally supporting the other.

Creative, hands-on activities further enriched these experiences. For Esperanza Rising, students created story quilts inspired by the events in Esperanza's life. Each patch represented a significant moment: a train for her journey to America, a rose for her father, and a pair of hands for the hard labor she endured. As they worked on their quilts, the students discussed the meanings behind their symbols, using new vocabulary and phrases they had learned from the text.

For *Tuck Everlasting*, we explored the theme of time by creating visual timelines of Winnie Foster's life choices, imagining what might have happened if she had chosen differently. Students eagerly debated the consequences of drinking from the magical spring, their arguments laced with evidence from the book. These projects allowed them to express their understanding in creative, tangible ways, breaking down language barriers and fostering a deeper appreciation for the stories.

The joy on their faces during these activities was unforgettable. I realized that literature had become more than just a tool for language learning—it was a gateway to self-expression, empathy, and confidence. My students were no longer passive readers; they were active participants, bringing their unique perspectives to each story we explored.

Reflecting on these moments, I am reminded of the power of literature to unite us, regardless of language or background. Stories like *Esperanza Rising* and *Tuck Everlasting* offer windows and mirrors—windows into other lives and experiences, and mirrors that reflect students' own identities and emotions.

When coupled with thoughtful activities and meaningful discussions, these novels can inspire ELs to see themselves not only as readers but as storytellers in their own right.

Incorporating novels like *Esperanza Rising* and *Tuck Everlasting* into the classroom demonstrates the incredible potential of literature to transform language learning into a deeply meaningful and joyous experience. By engaging with rich stories, students not only improve their reading and writing skills but also develop their voices, gain confidence, and foster empathy for others. Through activities like identifying verbs, creating descriptive sentences, and crafting story quilts or timelines, literature becomes a bridge between language development and creative self-expression.

As educators, we have the unique privilege of opening windows to new worlds while holding up mirrors that reflect students' own lives and experiences. When we thoughtfully combine literature with interactive and student-centered activities, we create a space where language learners can thrive—not just as students of a language, but as readers, writers, and storytellers. In this space, learning becomes not just a task, but a celebration of growth, connection, and discovery.

Let us continue to use the power of stories to inspire, teach, and connect, remembering that every word a student reads or writes brings them one step closer to finding their place in a world full of endless possibilities.

Teacher Tip

When introducing a novel to English Learners, it helps to break the story into smaller, manageable parts and pair each section with language-focused activities. For example, if you're reading Esperanza Rising, you might ask students to highlight or circle past-tense verbs in a particular chapter. Then, bring the class together to talk about how those verbs help tell the story. This kind of discussion not only builds grammar skills but also keeps students engaged with the plot. To deepen their connection with the book, try adding creative projects like visual timelines or story quilts. These activities invite students to express their understanding in personal and meaningful ways, making the learning process both powerful and enjoyable.

Parent Tip

Encourage your child to share the stories they're reading in class, even if they're still building confidence in English. Ask them about the characters, the plot, or any parts they find interesting or relatable.

If possible, read the book alongside them in your preferred language or in English to create a shared experience. Additionally, try to reinforce vocabulary or themes at home by relating them to everyday life. For example, if they're reading about family traditions in *Esperanza Rising*, talk about your own family traditions. This not only supports their learning but also strengthens your bond through meaningful conversations.

15 Empowering Readers to Pass High-stakes Exams

In today's world, Gen Z students are inundated with an overwhelming amount of information from digital platforms, ranging from social media posts to opinion pieces and news articles. This digital information landscape is often characterized by its rapid pace, lack of quality control, and potential for spreading misinformation. Research emphasizes that this shift in information consumption demands a corresponding shift in literacy education. According to the National Council of Teachers of English (NCTE), reading is no longer just about decoding and comprehending words on a page; It now Involves critical literacy, which empowers students to evaluate, analyze, and challenge the ideas presented in texts. A study by the Stanford History Education Group (2016) revealed that 82 percent of middle school students struggled to differentiate between ads and news stories labeled as "sponsored content," underscoring the need for explicit instruction in media literacy. Similarly, the International Literacy Association (ILA) emphasizes that critical reading skills are essential to help students discern fact from opinion and identify reliable sources in a digital environment where misinformation proliferates at alarming rates. Without explicit instruction in these skills, students are at risk of being manipulated by biased or false information, potentially undermining their ability to make informed decisions.

By teaching students to question, verify, and analyze what they read, educators prepare them to navigate this complex information landscape responsibly and confidently.

To prepare students for the reality of today's information-saturated world, explicit instruction in source evaluation is critical. Research underscores the importance of teaching students to consider authorship, intent, and evidence when engaging with any text. The Stanford History Education Group's "Civic

Online Reasoning" project (2016) highlights the pressing need for this kind of instruction, as their research found that most students lack the skills to assess online information effectively. For example, their study revealed that over two-thirds of high school students failed to question the credibility of a source based on its author's qualifications or potential biases. Media literacy scholars like Renee Hobbs advocate for integrating these skills into the classroom through targeted activities that teach students how to critically engage with information, especially when encountering sources on social media platforms. Hobbs argues that understanding the motivations behind information production, whether to inform, persuade, or profit, is essential for cultivating discerning readers.

In my classroom, I implement these research-backed strategies by asking students to examine the "who, what, why, and how" behind every text: Who wrote this? What is their perspective or potential bias? Why was this created, and how is the argument supported (or not supported) by evidence? These questions align with the CRAAP Test, a widely used evaluation tool that asks students to assess Currency, Relevance, Authority, Accuracy, and Purpose. By embedding these principles into reading exercises, I move beyond rote academic tasks to equip students with lifelong skills for engaging critically with information. As studies from the Pew Research Center (2020) emphasize, these skills are indispensable in a world where the lines between credible journalism and opinionated propaganda are often blurred. By teaching students to recognize biases and agendas behind the information they consume, I aim to create informed, thoughtful readers who can engage critically with the texts and ideas that shape their world.

One of the first strategies I teach is chunking, a powerful tool that helps students process and understand complex texts by breaking them down into smaller, more manageable parts. Chunking is particularly effective because it aligns with research on cognitive load theory, which suggests that the human brain can only process a limited amount of information at a time. By dividing a text into sections—whether by sentences, paragraphs, or key ideas—students can focus on understanding one segment at a time, reducing the risk of cognitive overload and frustration. This incremental approach also helps build confidence, as students tackle challenging content piece by piece rather than feeling overwhelmed by the text as a whole.

Beyond simplifying the reading process, chunking fosters active engagement with the material. After reading each section, students are encouraged to summarize the content in their own words, identify the main idea, or jot down any questions or connections that come to mind. For example, in a history lesson, students might break down a dense passage about the Civil Rights Movement into chunks that focus on key figures, events, and outcomes. After summarizing each chunk, they can identify recurring themes or evaluate the author's perspective on the subject. These activities not only reinforce comprehension but also encourage students to interact with the text critically and personally.

Mastering the skill of chunking is transformative for students, as it serves as a bridge from surface-level comprehension to deeper analysis. By understanding the smaller parts of a text, students are better equipped to see how they fit together as a whole, paving the way for evaluating the text's purpose, perspective, and credibility. In this way, chunking not only enhances reading comprehension but also lays the groundwork for developing critical literacy skills—skills that are essential for navigating complex academic texts and real-world information. Whether they are analyzing a persuasive essay, a scientific article, or a news report, chunking equips students with the tools to break down complexity and approach reading with confidence and curiosity.

To help students overcome the challenge of unfamiliar vocabulary, I teach them the FP'S BAG SALE strategy, created by Mark Pennington. This code-breaking technique empowers students to approach new words systematically, using context and their own knowledge to infer meanings.

By following these steps, they build confidence and independence, turning what might initially feel like an obstacle into a manageable and even rewarding part of the reading process.

FP'S BAG SALE: A Step-by-step Strategy

FP'S BAG SALE walks students through a series of techniques to decode unknown words:

Finish the Sentence: Read to the end of the sentence to see how the word fits.

Pronounce: Say the word out loud—sometimes it sounds like a familiar word.

Syllables: Break the word into smaller parts and see if any syllable looks familiar.

Before and After: Look at the sentences around the word for context clues.

Grammar: Identify the word's part of speech—knowing whether it's a noun, verb, or adjective can help narrow down its meaning.

Synonyms/Antonyms: Check if the sentence includes words that mean the same or the opposite.

Logic and Examples: Use the topic, logical reasoning, and examples in the text to deduce the meaning.

For example, when encountering the word "adversity" in a sentence like "They faced adversity during the harsh winter," students might follow the steps like this:

1 **Finish the Sentence:** The phrase "during the harsh winter" suggests hardship or struggle.

2 **Pronounce:** Saying the word out loud might remind them of words like adverse.

3 **Syllables:** Breaking it into ad-ver-si-ty might reveal recognizable parts, like adverse.

4 **Before and After:** Other sentences might describe the challenges people faced.

5 **Grammar:** Knowing it's a noun helps focus the meaning.

6 **Synonyms/Antonyms:** A comparison might show adversity means the opposite of comfort.

7 **Logic and Examples:** Harsh winters typically bring challenges, which support the inference.

Using this strategy, students often feel empowered to tackle unfamiliar words, especially during high-stakes exams when dictionaries aren't available. They learn not only to decode meanings but also to trust their intuition and reasoning skills. These small victories lay the groundwork for tackling more complex aspects of reading comprehension.

Credit

FP'S BAG SALE is a strategy developed by Mark Pennington and is used here with permission.

Exploring a Range of Reading Strategies

While FP'S BAG SALE equips students to decode challenging vocabulary, critical reading requires more than understanding individual words. To fully engage with a text, students need a range of strategies that help them identify main ideas, analyze purpose, and draw meaningful conclusions. Every reading passage I use is an opportunity to practice these critical skills, preparing students to apply them in various contexts, including high-stakes exams. Below are the key strategies we focus on:

- **Finding the Main Idea and Important Details:** To help students identify main ideas and supporting details, I often have them use two different colored highlighters: one for the main ideas and another for the details. For example, in a passage about climate change, students might highlight "rising global temperatures" as the main idea and "melting ice caps" or "increased droughts" as supporting evidence. Alternatively, I may cut the paragraphs into sections and have students work in groups to rearrange them, organizing the main idea and details into a logical sequence. This collaborative activity strengthens their understanding of text structure.

- **Drawing Conclusions and Making Predictions:** As we work through a passage, I encourage students to draw conclusions based on the information provided. For example, in a short story about a character facing adversity, students might infer the character's motivation or emotional state based on their actions. We also discuss what we can infer about themes or underlying messages.

  To develop predictive skills, students use evidence from the text to make predictions about what will happen next. For instance, in a narrative, they might predict a character's next decision based on prior actions or dialogue.

- **Comparing and Contrasting Ideas:** Comparing and contrasting ideas or characters help students think critically about the relationships within a text. I often use tools like Venn diagrams to visually organize similarities and differences. For instance, when comparing two characters in a story, students might note shared traits in the overlapping section while detailing unique qualities in separate areas.

- **Author's Purpose:** Identifying the author's purpose is crucial for understanding why a text was written. We analyze whether the author's intent is to inform, entertain, or persuade and discuss the evidence supporting their interpretation. For example, in an article advocating for recycling, students might highlight persuasive phrases or data as evidence of the author's goal to convince readers.
- **Fact vs. Opinion:** In informational texts, distinguishing between facts and opinions is a key skill. I model how to identify factual statements that can be verified, such as "The Amazon rainforest produces 20% of the world's oxygen," versus opinions like "Protecting the Amazon should be a global priority." Students practice this by highlighting or categorizing examples from the text.
- **Summarization:** Writing concise summaries helps students distill information and focus on the essentials. I model how to structure a summary using the beginning, middle, and end framework, focusing on the main idea and key details. For example, summarizing a passage on renewable energy might involve stating the main idea ("Renewable energy sources are crucial for sustainability") and listing supporting points like "solar power, wind energy, and hydropower as alternatives to fossil fuels."

By consistently practicing these strategies across different types of passages, students build a versatile toolkit for reading critically and strategically. These skills not only prepare them for exams but also enable them to engage meaningfully with the texts they encounter in everyday life.

Connecting Reading Strategies to STEM

Reading strategies like these are not only essential for literature and narrative texts but also play a critical role in STEM fields. In subjects like science, technology, engineering, and math, students often need to:

- **Analyze Complex Texts:** Whether it's scientific research, technical instructions, or mathematical explanations, students must be able to read and understand dense material.

- **Identify Key Concepts and Supporting Details:** Much like finding the main idea and details in a story, students must extract the core principles from STEM-related texts and use supporting evidence to understand theories or solve problems.
- **Make Predictions and Draw Conclusions:** In science, students regularly hypothesize and predict outcomes based on data or experiments. These skills mirror the predictive strategies used in reading fiction or informational texts.
- **Compare and Contrast Ideas:** STEM education often involves comparing experimental results or different technological approaches, similar to comparing and contrasting themes or characters in reading.
- **Understand the Author's Purpose:** In STEM, understanding why a researcher conducted an experiment or wrote a report (whether to inform, argue, or propose a solution) is critical for interpreting data and conclusions.
- **Fact vs. Opinion:** STEM fields rely heavily on distinguishing factual data from subjective opinions, particularly in research and real-world applications. Teaching students how to separate fact from opinion in reading passages strengthens their ability to critically assess information in science and technology.

For example, if we use a STEM-related passage about climate change research, students might:

- find the main idea about how climate change affects ecosystems
- draw conclusions about the data presented, making predictions about long-term environmental impacts
- compare and contrast different research methods or perspectives mentioned in the passage
- analyze the author's purpose, whether to inform about research findings or to persuade action on climate issues

By applying these reading strategies to STEM content, students not only improve their comprehension but also develop skills that are directly applicable to analyzing scientific reports, technical instructions, and data sets. This prepares them for high-stakes exams and for the critical reading and analysis they will encounter in STEM fields.

Assessing Students' Reading Skills

To assess students' understanding of these strategies, I use a combination of formative and summative assessments:

- **Formative Assessments** include having students highlight main ideas or make predictions in real time during lessons. Group discussions or peer feedback can also provide insight into how well students are applying the strategies.
- **Summative Assessments** can include quizzes, written summaries, or comprehension questions that require students to demonstrate mastery of the reading strategies independently.

By regularly checking for understanding and providing feedback, I ensure that students are making steady progress in mastering these critical reading skills.

Differentiation for Varied Proficiency Levels

Not all students will be ready to use these strategies at the same level. Here's how I differentiate:

- For **beginner** students, I focus on simpler strategies like finding the main idea or using context clues for unfamiliar words.
- For **intermediate** students, I incorporate more complex strategies like comparing and contrasting, drawing conclusions, and identifying the author's purpose.
- **Advanced** students may be asked to analyze multiple perspectives in a passage or synthesize information from several texts.
- This flexible approach ensures that every student is challenged but supported according to their proficiency level.

Student Reflection and Ownership

To encourage metacognitive awareness, I have students reflect on their use of reading strategies. After working through a passage, they answer questions like:

- "Which strategy helped you the most today?"

- "What was the hardest part of understanding this text?"
- "How did you use context clues to figure out new words?"

By reflecting on their learning, students develop a better understanding of their strengths and areas for improvement.

Conclusion

Consistency is key. Mastering reading strategies takes time and practice, but with consistent instruction and support, students can significantly improve their reading comprehension across subjects. Whether they are preparing for high-stakes exams or reading STEM-related texts, these strategies give students the tools they need to become independent, confident readers. With regular practice, feedback, and reflection, they are empowered to take on any reading challenge they encounter.

As students develop their reading skills, they naturally begin to notice the craft of writing, the way authors use vivid descriptions, carefully chosen words, and structured details to create meaning. This awareness is a powerful tool for teaching descriptive writing. Once students can identify the techniques authors use to paint pictures with words, they're ready to try it themselves.

In the next chapter, we'll explore how to teach descriptive writing to ELs, helping them bring their own stories, experiences, and ideas to life on the page. From crafting sensory-rich descriptions to developing their own voice, students will learn to use language as a tool for self-expression and creativity, just as they've seen in the texts they read.

Teacher Tip

Try to make reading strategy practice a regular part of your classroom, whether it's daily or weekly. The key is consistency. Using the same strategies across different subjects helps students get more comfortable and confident with them. Give students feedback along the way, and take time to let them reflect on what they're learning. Even a quick check-in can help them see how far they've come and encourage them to take more ownership of their reading.

Parent Tip

Support your child's reading in both your home language and English. Let them know it's okay to talk about the story in whichever language they feel most comfortable, it all helps them understand better.

You might ask questions in your home language like, "What's this story mostly about?" or "How would you say that in English?" This helps them make connections between both languages and grow as a reader. Just remember, reading in two languages takes time, so be patient. Your encouragement makes a big difference.

Part 4
Empowering English Learners and Teachers for Success

16 **Unlocking Potential**

Every student who walks into a classroom brings with them a world of stories, layers of experience, emotion, and identity that shape how they see themselves and the world around them. Some carry quiet confidence, while others come burdened by challenges that aren't always visible. Behind academic struggles or behavioral outbursts, there's often a deeper story, one of untapped potential hidden beneath years of self-doubt, unmet expectations, or painful comparisons.

As teachers, our role is much more than delivering lessons. We're here to see each student for who they are, to help them break through the walls they've built, and to remind them of the strength they may have forgotten they had.

Saul's Journey: Finding His Voice

One student I'll never forget is Saul. He arrived in my classroom quiet, withdrawn, and clearly weighed down by years of being compared to his older brother, someone known for his academic success and glowing reputation. Saul, on the other hand, barely spoke in class, kept his head down, and often fell asleep at his desk. It would have been easy to label him as uninterested or lazy. But I knew there was more to his story.

I could see that Saul wasn't just struggling with schoolwork, he was struggling with himself. The comparisons had dimmed his light, and by the time he landed in my class, he seemed to have given up on trying to shine at all.

I started with simple steps: short conversations, asking him about his interests, trying to make a connection without pressure. Slowly, he began to open up. That's when I learned about his love for playing the guitar. His whole face changed when he talked about music; there was a spark, small but undeniable.

So one day, I gently asked if he'd be willing to bring his guitar to school and play something for the class. He was hesitant, afraid of judgment, unsure of himself, but eventually, he said yes.

When the moment came, something incredible happened. Saul stepped to the front of the room, guitar in hand, and as he began to play, the entire class went silent. In that moment, he wasn't the "quiet kid" or "the underachiever"— he was a musician, confident and present. We saw him differently, and more importantly, he saw himself differently too.

That moment didn't fix everything overnight, but it was a turning point. It reminded me why I do this work. Every student has a light, even if it's buried deep. And it's our job to help them find it, nurture it, and let it shine.

Saul's story isn't unique, it's one of many that have shaped who I am as an educator. Teaching isn't just about academics; it's about helping students believe in themselves again. Because when they do, that's when real learning begins.

Though his grades didn't improve immediately, I could see that something had shifted within him. The small act of recognizing and celebrating his talent had ignited a spark. His confidence grew, and he began to approach his schoolwork with a renewed sense of determination. Encouraged by his progress, one of the school administrators proposed giving Saul a certificate to acknowledge his effort and growth. Initially, some teachers hesitated, skeptical of rewarding what they saw as minimal improvement. But we all agreed that even small steps deserved recognition.

When Saul received his certificate, the effect was transformative. His eyes brimmed with pride as he held the acknowledgment of his hard work. From that moment on, something clicked. Saul became one of the most diligent students in the class, tackling assignments with enthusiasm and showing a newfound commitment to his learning. His grades improved steadily, but more importantly, his attitude shifted completely. He had rediscovered his sense of self-worth, and with it, a belief in his own potential.

Saul's journey was a powerful reminder that every student carries hidden strengths, waiting to be nurtured. Sometimes, all it takes is a moment of recognition and a little faith to reignite the light within.

Educational Strategy: Encouraging Student Interest

Teachers can unlock student potential by:

1 **Identifying Interests:** Take the time to learn about what excites and motivates each student, whether it's music, sports, or other hobbies.

2 **Providing Opportunities for Expression:** Allow students to showcase their talents in ways that connect to the classroom, whether through presentations, performances, or creative projects.

3 **Celebrating Effort and Progress:** Recognize students' efforts, not just their academic achievements, to foster a sense of pride and self-worth.

Saul's story reminded me that every student's challenges are unique, and unlocking their potential often requires a tailored approach. Just as Saul needed support to rediscover his spark, other students, like Ziyad and Sarah, faced their own hurdles. Their story highlights the importance of empathy and collaboration when helping students navigate difficult transitions

Supporting Students in Difficult Transitions: Ziyad and Sarah

Ziyad and Sarah, siblings from Saudi Arabia, arrived in my classroom carrying more than just the weight of learning a new language. Their quiet demeanor and downcast gazes reflected deeper struggles: adjusting to an unfamiliar educational system, grappling with their mother's illness, and navigating the cultural shift of moving to a co-educational school environment. Ziyad, in particular, found mixed-gender classrooms uncomfortable, which added another layer of complexity to their transition.

Recognizing their vulnerability, I knew that a one-size-fits-all approach wouldn't suffice. I worked closely with their content area teachers to adapt lessons and provide scaffolding that allowed them to engage with the curriculum without feeling overwhelmed. These adjustments included simplifying texts, integrating visuals to support comprehension, and providing opportunities for small-group work where they felt safer participating. I also made it a point to create a welcoming classroom atmosphere, one where their cultural values and experiences were acknowledged and respected.

To support Ziyad and Sarah emotionally, I took time to build trust, ensuring they felt heard and understood. During our one-on-one sessions, I encouraged them to share their thoughts and feelings at their own pace, often using prompts that connected with their cultural and personal experiences. For instance, I asked them to write about traditions or memories from home, which not only gave them a chance to express themselves but also helped them practice English in a meaningful way.

Over time, I began to see small but significant changes. Ziyad started raising his hand during group discussions, and Sarah's shy smile grew more frequent as she gained confidence in her reading skills. These moments were a testament to their resilience and the power of a supportive learning environment.

This impact was echoed in a letter I received from their mother before she passed away. In it, she expressed profound gratitude for the support her children received during such a difficult year. She wrote about how Ziyad and Sarah had grown not only in their English proficiency but also in their confidence and mindset toward learning. Her words reflected the value of patience, cultural understanding, and the importance of educators who recognize each child's emotional and academic needs.

Ziyad and Sarah's journey was a reminder that education is not just about imparting knowledge but also about creating spaces where students feel safe, valued, and empowered to overcome their challenges.

Educational Strategy: Supporting Students with Personal and Cultural Challenges

To help students like Ziyad and Sarah, teachers can:

- **Collaborate with Colleagues:** Work with other teachers to create a consistent and supportive approach across subjects.
- **Modify Curriculum and Assessments:** Provide additional resources and adjust assignments to ensure that students can succeed despite language barriers.
- **Offer Emotional Support:** Recognize the personal challenges students may be facing and create a classroom environment that is emotionally supportive and understanding.

While Ziyad and Sarah's story demonstrates the importance of cultural sensitivity and addressing external challenges, every student's journey is unique, shaped by their own set of circumstances. Some students face external pressures, while others battle internal struggles, such as self-doubt or the weight of high expectations. Yingting's story is a testament to the significance of emotional support in helping students overcome these internal barriers and discover their potential. Just as Ziyad and Sarah needed a culturally responsive approach, Yingting required encouragement and understanding to thrive academically and emotionally.

Supporting Students with Emotional Barriers

Just as Ziyad and Sarah's story highlighted the importance of addressing cultural and personal challenges, Yingting's journey demonstrates the significance of providing emotional support. While each student's needs are unique, the common thread lies in understanding and addressing their specific barriers to learning.

Yingting's Story

Yingting was a brilliant and hardworking student who approached her studies with dedication and determination. She made remarkable progress in improving her English, but there was one subject that filled her with dread: Science. Despite her overall academic success, Yingting was convinced that she lacked the ability to excel in Science. One afternoon, she came to my classroom in tears, overwhelmed by the thought of an upcoming Science exam.

As we talked, I realized that her struggle wasn't academic; she had already mastered the necessary vocabulary and concepts for her Science lessons. Her challenge was emotional; she doubted her own abilities and allowed her anxiety to overshadow her knowledge. Determined to help her, I offered to review the material with her after school.

During our session, Yingting hesitantly worked through the questions, and to her surprise, and mine, she answered them with confidence and accuracy. It became clear that she didn't need additional academic instruction; she needed someone to remind her of her capabilities and help her see the brilliance she already possessed. Together, we discussed strategies for managing her anxiety and reframed the exam as an opportunity to showcase what she had learned.

When the exam day came, Yingting walked into the classroom with renewed confidence, and her performance reflected it. She didn't just pass the exam—she excelled. Watching her smile as she shared her results was one of the most rewarding moments of my teaching career.

Years later, I received a letter from Yingting, one I treasure to this day. In it, she reflected on the moment that had transformed her perspective on herself and her abilities. She thanked me not only for the academic support but for believing in her when she couldn't believe in herself.

"Dear Mrs. Elbaz,

I still remember the first day I stepped into your ESL class in 6th grade. I didn't know much English, and I was really nervous and shy, but you were so friendly. You asked about my name, my age, and where I came from. Your thoughtfulness and kindness really made me love that class … You're not only a teacher to me; you're like a mom to me."

This letter confirmed for me that our work as teachers goes beyond academics. Sometimes, the greatest gift we can give our students is belief in themselves.

Educational Strategy: Providing Emotional Support

To help students unlock their potential, teachers can:

1 **Address Emotional Barriers:** Recognize when a student's struggles are emotional rather than academic, and provide the reassurance they need to succeed.
2 **Encourage Self-confidence:** Offer positive reinforcement and help students see their own strengths, particularly when they doubt themselves.
3 **Foster a Growth Mindset:** Teach students that intelligence and abilities can grow with effort and persistence, helping them view challenges as opportunities for growth.

Dear Mrs. Elbaz:

Hi Mrs. Elbaz, I still remember the first day I stepped in to your ESL class in 6th grade. I didn't know much English, and I was really nervous and shy, but you were so friendly. You asked about my name, my age, and where did I came from. Your thoughtfulness and kindness really made me love that class. From then, you became my #1 favorite teacher on my favorite teacher list. Even till now, you are still on my #1 favorite teacher list. Every time I had a problem, you were always there and figure out the problem for me. From the bottom of my heart, you're not only a teacher to me, not only a friend to me. You're like a mom to me.

When I move to high school next year, I will miss the #1 teacher (Mrs. Elbaz). I hope we can stay in touch.

Also wish you a MERRY CHRISTMAS and a HAPPY NEW YEAR!

P.S. I hope you like my present. ♥

— Yingting

Figure 16.1 Yingting's handwritten letter reflecting on the encouragement she received in her first year of learning English, highlighting the lasting bond between teacher and student. © Tiffany Liu, used with permission.

In 2025, I received a touching message from Yingting. She shared that she had become a dental hygienist, a career she loves and takes great pride in. What moved me most was her heartfelt request to use her original name in my book. "I love my original name so much, and it would be amazing if that can appear in your book," she wrote. Her words were a beautiful reminder of how far she had come—not only in mastering a new language, but in embracing her identity with confidence and pride.

Yingting's story is a powerful testament to the lasting impact of culturally responsive teaching. It shows how supporting a student's voice, heritage, and emotional growth can shape their sense of self long after they leave our classrooms. Messages like hers reaffirm that teaching is not only about academic progress but also about believing in each student's potential and honoring who they are becoming.

Yingting's journey, like Saul's, reminds me of a vital truth: students' success often hinges not just on their intellectual abilities, but on their emotional readiness to embrace challenges.

The Power of Emotional Support

Through experiences like those with Saul and Yingting, I've come to deeply appreciate the transformative power of emotional support in education. Students often struggle not because they lack ability, but because they lack the confidence to believe in their own potential. This is where developing a growth mindset becomes essential. By helping students understand that their abilities can grow with effort and perseverance, we enable them to see challenges as opportunities rather than roadblocks.

Emotional support is not about removing obstacles; it's about equipping students with the resilience and belief that they can overcome them. Encouraging students to view setbacks as a natural part of the learning process fosters an environment where mistakes are not feared but embraced as tools for growth. In my own classroom, I've seen how this approach can transform hesitant learners into determined individuals who no longer shy away from challenges, but instead approach them with curiosity and confidence.

Building Strong Teacher–Student Relationships

Unlocking a student's potential begins with fostering meaningful and authentic relationships that go beyond academics. When educators take the time to see their students as individuals rather than just grades or test scores, they lay the groundwork for trust and mutual respect. Each student carries with them a unique story shaped by their experiences, dreams, and struggles. For students like Saul and Yingting, it was this relational connection that became the key to understanding and addressing their needs, empowering them to overcome obstacles and thrive.

Building such connections requires time, patience, and an unwavering commitment to seeing the whole child. It involves observing their actions, listening to their concerns, and finding entry points to connect with their interests or passions. With Saul, it was music that created the bridge; with Yingting, it was reassurance and emotional support. These moments of connection, though seemingly small, communicate to students that they are seen, valued, and supported. They convey to students that their teacher genuinely believes in their ability to succeed, a belief that often becomes a self-fulfilling prophecy.

When students trust that their teacher cares for them as individuals, they begin to let down their guard, allowing for deeper engagement with their learning. This trust transforms the classroom into a safe space where students feel empowered to take risks, make mistakes, and explore their potential without fear of judgment. Over time, these strong teacher–student relationships contribute to a classroom culture where students not only achieve academic success but also develop the confidence, resilience, and self-awareness needed to navigate challenges in all areas of their lives.

Educational Strategy: Building Trust with Students

To build strong relationships with students, teachers can:

1 **Listen Actively:** Take the time to understand students' concerns, interests, and motivations.

2 **Show Empathy:** Acknowledge their challenges and provide support both academically and emotionally.

3 **Be Consistent:** Maintain trust by being reliable, encouraging, and fair in your interactions with students.

Conclusion: The Collective Journey to Unlocking Potential

Unlocking a student's potential is a shared responsibility that requires seeing beyond academic performance to nurture the whole individual. It starts with recognizing and celebrating each student's unique strengths, whether those strengths are talents, cultural perspectives, or personal stories that shape their identity. Just as important is providing emotional support to guide students through challenges, whether they stem from academic struggles, personal circumstances, or a lack of confidence.

Fostering a growth mindset in students is essential to helping them believe in their ability to improve and succeed. When students view challenges not as obstacles but as opportunities for growth, they develop resilience and the courage to take risks in their learning. This transformation cannot happen in isolation, it requires collaboration among teachers, parents, and students themselves. By building partnerships and creating an inclusive, supportive environment, we empower students to overcome barriers, embrace their potential, and thrive both inside and outside the classroom.

As educators, our role extends far beyond delivering content; we are mentors, advocates, and guides on our students' journeys. By listening to their stories, acknowledging their struggles, and celebrating their progress, we help them see the value in their unique contributions to the world. Together, through collective effort and unwavering belief in their potential, we pave the way for students to become confident, capable individuals who are prepared to take on any challenge they encounter.

Teacher Tip

Go beyond assessing academic performance and take time to understand each student's unique background, interests, and challenges. Recognize that success isn't solely measured by grades, but by growth and resilience. Foster a growth mindset by celebrating not just achievements but also effort and progress, no matter how small. Tailor your support to individual needs, whether it's through one-on-one encouragement, hands-on learning opportunities, or creative outlets that allow students to explore their strengths. By creating a safe and supportive environment where students feel valued, you empower them to discover abilities they may not realize they possess, building their confidence and setting them on a path to success.

Parent Tip

Help your child discover their strengths by encouraging them to try new activities and take on challenges. Focus on their effort and progress rather than just the end result, and remind them that making mistakes is part of learning. Your positive reinforcement can build their confidence and motivate them to keep growing, both academically and personally.

17 Meeting the Specific Needs of Students

I remember one particular day when I was standing in front of my class, preparing to start a lesson. Suddenly, I noticed two middle-aged men standing by the door, wearing visitor badges. One of them glanced at the "ESL" sign hanging on my classroom door and smiled warmly. "I'm so glad they have these classes now in the USA," he said, his voice tinged with nostalgia.

Curious, I asked him why it meant so much to him. He paused for a moment, and then replied with a bittersweet smile:

> When I moved to Houston with my parents a long time ago, speaking Spanish was prohibited by law. My father used to hit me if I spoke in Spanish because he was afraid I'd get into trouble. There were no classes like this back then, no support for students like me. That's why I'm so glad to see this class here, right in the heart of a school.

His words struck me deeply, and I felt a wave of gratitude for the progress that had been made in creating inclusive educational spaces. It was a powerful reminder of how important it is to provide a safe environment where students can embrace their identities and learn without fear. It reinforced my commitment to meeting the specific needs of each student, ensuring they felt seen, valued, and supported in their journey.

Going Beyond the Lesson Plan: The Role of Empathy in Education

This moment brought to mind a valuable conversation I had with the ESL coordinator of our district. She shared with me that her very first teaching post was in a remote village along the American-Canadian border. In that elementary school, many of the children came to class without having brushed their teeth. It wasn't written anywhere in her job contract, but she quickly realized that if she wanted to address their needs effectively, she had to care about more than just academics. So, she made it a part of their daily routine to brush their teeth at school. "Was this written in my job contract?" she asked rhetorically. "No, but as teachers, we attend to the specific needs of students because we care."

Her story resonated with me, reinforcing the idea that teaching is about so much more than lesson plans or academic goals. It's about recognizing and responding to the needs that our students bring into the classroom, even if they fall outside the usual expectations of our role.

Educational Strategy: Responding to the Whole Child

Addressing the holistic development of students, encompassing their physical, emotional, social, and academic needs, is essential for fostering well-rounded individuals prepared for life's challenges. This comprehensive approach, often referred to as educating the "whole child," is supported by extensive research highlighting its benefits. Recognizing that students bring their entire selves into the classroom is fundamental. Their physical health, emotional states, and social backgrounds significantly influence their learning experiences. Research indicates that when educators acknowledge and address these multifaceted needs, students exhibit improved engagement and academic performance. A report by the Learning Policy Institute emphasizes that a whole child approach, which attends to students' comprehensive developmental needs, leads to better educational outcomes. This perspective underscores the importance of understanding students as individuals, not just learners.

Flexibility in teaching is crucial for meeting the diverse challenges students face, many of which extend beyond academic concerns. Teachers who adapt their approaches to individual circumstances foster more inclusive and supportive learning environments. Studies have shown that such adaptability enhances students' social and emotional skills, which are critical for overall development. For instance, a systematic review highlighted that social and emotional learning (SEL) interventions in schools have a positive impact on students' social behaviors and reduce conduct problems, reinforcing the need for flexible, student-centered teaching. Empathy is the cornerstone of meaningful teacher–student relationships. When educators demonstrate genuine care, they create environments of trust and support where students feel valued. Research underscores that students in nurturing environments develop stronger social-emotional skills, which are linked to academic success and well-being. A meta-analysis of SEL programs found that participants showed significant improvements in social behaviors, emotional regulation, and academic performance, highlighting the importance of empathetic teaching practices.

Incorporating SEL into the curriculum equips students with essential life skills such as self-awareness, emotional regulation, and interpersonal abilities. These competencies are vital for navigating both personal and academic challenges. Research from the Education Endowment Foundation suggests that effective SEL interventions lead to an average of four months' additional progress in academic outcomes. Furthermore, fostering SEL ensures that students are better prepared to handle stress, build relationships, and approach learning with confidence. By adopting a holistic approach that integrates SEL, educators not only support students academically but also nurture their emotional and social well-being. This strategy lays the foundation for lifelong success, empowering students to thrive both inside and outside the classroom.

Kevin's Story

One of the most memorable challenges I faced was with a Grade 7 student named Kevin, who often appeared uninterested and distracted in my ESL class. I knew he had Attention-Deficit/Hyperactivity Disorder (ADHD), and I had heard more than one teacher complain about his behavior. Many had already labeled him as a "troublemaker," but I decided not to have any preconceived ideas. Instead, I approached him with an open mind, determined to understand his specific needs.

Through experience, I learned that when students' needs aren't met, they often act up or seem disengaged. This is especially true for (ELs, who might develop behavior problems if the language used in academic content classes is too difficult for them to understand. When students are overwhelmed by language barriers, they may feel frustrated or disconnected, which can manifest as disruptive behavior. However, when they are involved in meaningful activities and feel understood, their behavior can improve a great deal.

This was precisely the case with Kevin. After having a private conversation with him, I realized that his restlessness wasn't a sign of defiance but rather a way of coping with his need for movement. We agreed that he could move around quietly whenever necessary, as long as it didn't disrupt the class. This simple adjustment made a world of difference. Kevin became more engaged in class activities, and his behavior transformed. By meeting his needs and helping him self-regulate, I was also fostering key SEL skills like self-awareness and self-management.

Two years later, while I was teaching, Kevin returned to my classroom with a proud smile. He pulled out a bookmark I had once given him as a reward during a class competition and said, "I've kept this with me ever since you gave it to me." That moment reminded me that small gestures of recognition and understanding can have lasting impacts on students' lives. Kevin's story taught me that what may seem like misbehavior is often a student's way of communicating an unmet need, and that addressing those needs with empathy can transform both behavior and learning outcomes.

Educational Strategy: Supporting Students with ADHD

To meet the needs of students like Kevin, teachers can create a more inclusive and supportive learning environment by employing strategies that prioritize flexibility and recognition of individual strengths. Traditional classroom rules often emphasize structure and predictability, which can pose challenges for students with ADHD who struggle with impulse control, sustained attention, or the ability to sit still for long periods. Adapting these rules to accommodate specific needs can make a significant difference. For instance, allowing Kevin to move around quietly when needed empowered him to self-regulate without disrupting the class or feeling like he was breaking rules. Simple adjustments like these give students the tools to succeed, while respecting the overall classroom environment. Teachers can also introduce tools such as fidget toys, standing desks, or scheduled movement breaks, which can provide students with alternative ways to stay engaged.

Recognizing and celebrating effort rather than focusing solely on outcomes is another essential strategy. Students with ADHD often experience frustration or discouragement when their struggles overshadow their achievements.

By celebrating small victories, such as completing a task, contributing to a discussion, or showing improved focus, teachers can help these students build confidence and motivation. Positive reinforcement systems, such as verbal praise or tangible rewards, can reinforce a sense of progress and accomplishment. For Kevin, something as simple as a bookmark became a lasting symbol of recognition, reminding him that his efforts were valued and appreciated.

Equally important is focusing on students' strengths and passions. Many students with ADHD excel in areas that require creativity, problem-solving, or hands-on learning. Teachers who take the time to identify these strengths and incorporate them into lessons can transform how students see themselves and their capabilities. For instance, if Kevin had a passion for technology or storytelling, designing assignments that allowed him to use those skills could have made his learning experience more meaningful and enjoyable. This approach not only builds self-esteem but also creates a stronger connection to the material being taught.

Finally, collaborating with students to develop their own accommodations can increase their sense of ownership and responsibility. When Kevin and his teacher worked together to agree on how he could manage his restlessness, he felt respected and supported, which encouraged him to self-regulate. This collaborative approach empowers students to self-advocate and equips them with tools to navigate similar challenges in the future.

In practice, these strategies can be embedded into daily classroom routines to benefit all students, not just those with ADHD. For example, in a flexible classroom environment, students could choose to work standing up, take breaks to stretch or walk, or participate in interactive, movement-based activities. These small adjustments create a dynamic, student-centered classroom where all learners feel supported in reaching their full potential.

To Meet the Needs of Students Like Kevin, Teachers Can

- **Adapt Classroom Rules:** Allow flexibility in how students meet expectations, such as permitting movement for students who need it to stay focused.

- **Recognize Effort:** Celebrate small victories and acknowledge effort to build students' self-esteem.
- **Focus on Strengths:** Identify and emphasize what each student does well, even if it's outside the traditional academic measures.

Ahixa's Story: Breaking Language Barriers with Compassion

When Ahixa came to my classroom, she was overwhelmed. As a newcomer from Honduras, she spoke very little English and the language barrier made her visibly anxious. Her initial response to this unfamiliar environment was to retreat into herself—she avoided eye contact, rarely spoke, and stayed quiet during group activities. It wasn't that she lacked the desire to participate; she simply didn't know how to bridge the gap between her thoughts and the English language.

From the start, I knew that Ahixa's path to success would require patience and gentle guidance. I began by introducing visuals and gestures during lessons to help make the content more accessible for her. Whether it was a simple diagram or acting out instructions, I made sure that every new concept was supported by something she could relate to visually. This allowed Ahixa to connect with the lessons without having to rely solely on language, reducing her frustration and helping her feel less isolated.

Recognizing the importance of peer support, I paired Ahixa with a bilingual peer mentor, a student who spoke both Spanish and English. This mentor became a bridge for Ahixa—translating instructions when needed but more importantly modeling how to engage in classroom activities and discussions. Gradually, Ahixa began to open up, responding to questions with simple gestures or one-word answers in English. These small victories were celebrated in the classroom, encouraging her to push forward.

Then, one day during a reading exercise, Ahixa took a significant step. She tentatively raised her hand and volunteered to read a sentence aloud. Though her voice trembled with nervousness, she completed the sentence, and the class erupted in applause. That moment was pivotal for her—it marked the beginning of her journey from a quiet observer to an active participant in her own learning.

Over the course of the next year, Ahixa's progress was remarkable. She grew more confident, participating in class discussions, working in groups, and even helping peers during activities. Her growing proficiency in English wasn't just apparent through her verbal participation—it was measurable. At the end of the school year, her test scores reflected the strides she had made.

Ahixa's Progress in Numbers

One year after joining the class, Ahixa's reading and writing proficiency had significantly improved. Her reading DRA2 score was 40—a clear indicator of her growing ability to comprehend texts. In the TELPAS (Texas English Language Proficiency Assessment System) scores, she achieved an advanced high rating in listening, speaking, and writing. This advanced proficiency level showed that not only was she understanding English, but she was also able to express herself fluently and effectively across multiple language domains.

Reflection on Ahixa's Growth

Ahixa's journey is a reminder of the transformative power of consistent support and high expectations. Her progress, from that of a hesitant student to a confident and engaged learner, illustrates how essential it is to create a nurturing environment where students feel empowered to take risks. Her final scores were a testament not just to her hard work, but to the collective efforts of the classroom community that helped her thrive. With the right support, Ahixa broke through the language barriers that once held her back and exceeded even my highest expectations.

Teacher Tip

One of the most effective ways to meet the specific needs of students is to build authentic relationships with them. Take time to learn about their lives, cultures, and unique challenges. For example, Kevin's story reminds us that labels like "troublemaker" often mask underlying needs. By understanding the whole child, you can adapt your teaching approach to create an environment where they feel valued and supported. A simple strategy is to hold regular one-on-one check-ins with students, giving them space to share their concerns or successes. Even small gestures, like asking about their weekend or attending a school event they're involved in, can strengthen the teacher–student bond and enhance their engagement in learning.

Parent Tip

As a parent, you play a key role in helping your child thrive in school by supporting their academic and emotional needs. Encourage open communication with their teachers, as this partnership is vital for addressing any challenges your child might face. For example, if your child has ADHD or struggles with focus, share specific strategies that work at home so the teacher can apply them in the classroom. At home, foster a safe space where your child feels comfortable talking about their school experiences. Celebrate their progress, no matter how small, and remind them that their growth matters more than perfection. This support helps them build confidence and resilience both in and outside the classroom.

Part 5
Advanced Tools for Classroom Innovation

18 Cultivating Growth: Building Skills as an Educator

Although the district only required fourteen hours of staff development each year, I found myself diving into far more, eager to soak up everything I could. In one of my early years, I completed over 80 hours of training. I was hungry to grow. To me, it felt like a gift that so many professional learning opportunities were available, and I wanted to take full advantage. These sessions didn't just sharpen my teaching skills—they shaped the way I saw my role in the classroom. I remember meeting a fellow teacher at one of these sessions who offered a piece of advice I've never forgotten: "Stay away from negative people." At the time, it seemed simple. But over the years, I've come to realize how powerful that wisdom truly is. Teaching is emotionally demanding, and choosing to stay close to uplifting voices helped me stay grounded, focused, and open to learning. That mindset, of actively seeking out both knowledge and positivity, has remained a guiding principle throughout my career.

As I transitioned into my teaching role, it quickly became clear that learning didn't end with my degree. In fact, the real education began the moment I stepped into the classroom, where every day presented a new challenge and an opportunity to grow. My journey as a teacher was shaped not only by the experiences I shared with my students but also by the invaluable staff development sessions that exposed me to a wide range of strategies, philosophies, and insights. These sessions became a cornerstone of my growth, providing me with the tools to navigate the complexities of teaching in a multicultural and multilingual classroom.

One of the most transformative experiences was learning about the SIOP (Sheltered Instruction Observation Protocol) model. The SIOP model provided me with a structured and research-based approach to teaching English learners, emphasizing strategies that made content comprehensible while simultaneously building language skills. It consists of eight key components: lesson preparation, building background, comprehensible input, strategies, interaction, practice/application, lesson delivery, and review/assessment. Each of these components played a vital role in helping me create lessons that were not only accessible but also engaging for my students.

By integrating SIOP techniques, such as using visuals, realia, and gestures to support comprehension (Comprehensible Input), I made complex content more understandable for my students. Additionally, I focused on building background knowledge by connecting lessons to students' prior experiences, which allowed them to make meaningful connections to the material. Hands-on activities became a staple in my classroom, as they provided opportunities for students to practice new vocabulary and concepts actively, while structured group interactions encouraged them to communicate and collaborate with their peers.

One of the most impactful aspects of the SIOP model was the emphasis on student interaction. I implemented strategies that promoted student-to-student dialogue, such as think-pair-share and jigsaw activities, which gave every student a chance to participate. This interactive approach helped students practice language skills in a supportive environment, boosting their confidence and willingness to contribute to class discussions.

As I consistently incorporated these SIOP techniques into my teaching, I noticed a significant transformation in my classroom. My students became more engaged, and I could see their language skills improving as they felt comfortable participating in class discussions, expressing their ideas, and taking ownership of their learning. The SIOP model not only made my lessons more dynamic but also provided a framework that ensured I was meeting the diverse linguistic and academic needs of my English learners.

A pivotal moment in my professional development was when I explored Noam Chomsky's revolutionary theories on language acquisition and cognitive development. His concept of a universal grammar—that humans possess an innate ability to learn and generate language—challenged me to rethink my approach to teaching English learners. Chomsky's emphasis on the innate structures of the mind and the creative potential of language inspired me to move beyond rote memorization and focus on fostering my students' ability to construct meaning and express themselves fluently. This shift fundamentally transformed my teaching philosophy, encouraging me to create an environment where students could engage with language in dynamic, authentic ways, unlocking their potential as confident and independent communicators.

Building on this, Bloom's Taxonomy provided a practical framework to apply these ideas in the classroom. The taxonomy's hierarchy of cognitive skills, ranging from basic recall and comprehension to more advanced abilities such as analysis, synthesis, and evaluation, helped me design lessons that challenged students to think critically and creatively. For example, I began incorporating activities that required them to draw conclusions, make inferences, and apply their knowledge to solve real-world problems. This alignment between Chomsky's theoretical insights and Bloom's practical framework reinforced my belief that true learning occurs when students are encouraged to forge connections between ideas and concepts on a deeper level. By integrating these approaches, I shifted from simply teaching content to empowering my students to become independent, analytical thinkers.

Drawing from this experience, another transformative moment came when I attended a workshop called "Gifted and Talented," conducted by Dr. Terry Brandt. Although the workshop was designed for teachers who specialized in gifted and talented education, I was keen to attend, even though it wouldn't count toward my Continuing Professional Development (CPD). I believed that many of my EL students were gifted and talented in their own right; they simply lacked the language proficiency to express their abilities. Dr. Brandt wasn't an expert in language teaching, but his insights were universal in their application.

During the workshop, Dr. Brandt introduced a concept that fundamentally changed how I approached teaching projects. He emphasized that showing students a model of a project could unintentionally limit their creativity, as they might feel compelled to replicate the example rather than exploring their own ideas. Instead, he advocated for providing students with a clear rubric that outlined expectations, thereby granting them the freedom to interpret the assignment in their unique way. This insight resonated deeply with me, and from that day forward, I consciously stopped showing my students examples of "perfect" projects.

The impact of this change was profound. By allowing my students, the freedom to explore and create without predefined constraints, I observed an incredible surge in originality and enthusiasm. They began to take ownership of their projects, using their cultural backgrounds, personal experiences, and newfound language skills to produce work that was not only creative but also richly diverse in perspective. It was a joy to see how they applied higher order thinking skills—evaluating different approaches, synthesizing information from various sources, and making connections to broader themes—through projects that truly reflected their individuality. This experience reaffirmed my belief that, when given the opportunity to think critically and express themselves authentically, every student has the potential to exceed expectations, regardless of language proficiency.

As I continued my journey, I was introduced to Vygotsky's concept of the Zone of Proximal Development (ZPD). This theory highlighted the importance of providing students with tasks that were just beyond their current abilities, supporting them as they moved from what they could do independently to what they could achieve with guidance. Vygotsky emphasized that with the right amount of support or "scaffolding," students could gradually master more complex skills, building their confidence and competence.

To implement this in my classroom, I often drew a visual of the "I do, We do, You do" instructional model to guide my students through the learning process. This approach allowed me to demonstrate a task first ("I do"), then work through it together with my students ("We do"), and finally, encourage them to complete it independently ("You do"). By using this method, I ensured that students were gradually stepping out of their comfort zones, tackling challenges with the right level of support until they felt confident enough to succeed on their own.

For example, when teaching writing, I might start by modeling how to structure a paragraph ("I do"), then engage the class in crafting a paragraph together ("We do"), and eventually, have them write their own with minimal guidance ("You do"). In reading activities, I paired more advanced students with those who needed help, allowing them to guide their peers through challenging texts, fostering a collaborative learning environment.

As a result, I saw my students becoming more confident in tackling challenges they had initially thought were beyond their capabilities. They began to take more risks in their learning, knowing that they had the support they needed to succeed. This approach not only improved their academic skills but also nurtured a growth mindset, as they started to believe in their ability to overcome obstacles and make progress. It was incredibly rewarding to witness their excitement when they realized they could accomplish something they once thought was too difficult, and it reinforced my belief in the power of guided learning to unlock every student's potential.

Additionally, I attended sessions on Literacy Through Photography (LTP), where I learned how to use photographs as a tool for language development. This approach was particularly effective in helping students articulate their thoughts and ideas, as they could describe, analyze, and create stories based on images. When I introduced this method in class, I saw even my most reluctant writers eagerly describe the scenes in the photographs, which led to richer vocabulary usage and more expressive writing.

I also used LTP to teach students how their camera's focus could change their point of view, depending on how they saw a topic and from which angle they held their camera. This exercise not only allowed them to explore different perspectives but also helped them understand that their interpretation of a subject could vary greatly, just as their writing could take on different layers of meaning. It was a powerful way to show them that their voice mattered and that they had the ability to express their unique perspective, both visually and in writing.

Furthermore, photos became a great tool for improving students' listening and speaking skills. I would put up a photo and ask them what they saw, allowing them to use whatever language they had to describe the image. This created a non-threatening environment where students felt comfortable interacting, making it easier for them to express their thoughts and ideas without fear of making mistakes. As they shared their observations, their confidence grew, and their language skills developed more naturally.

Staff development wasn't just about learning new techniques; it was also an opportunity to connect with other educators, share ideas, and learn from their experiences. During one workshop, I met an ESL teacher who had created a parents' night where her English learners explained what they were doing in class using their native language. This idea inspired me to find ways to involve parents in their children's education, recognizing that a strong home-school connection could make a world of difference in a student's success.

In addition, I attended Gretchen Bernabei's Writing Workshops, which emphasized the importance of teaching writing through storytelling and real-life experiences. Her approach was rooted in the belief that students write best when they have something meaningful to say, and this idea resonated deeply with me. The workshops introduced various techniques, such as the use of kernel essays, short, structured essays based on real-life events, and writing prompts that encouraged students to draw from their personal experiences. This method shifted the focus from the mechanics of writing to the act of sharing authentic stories, making the writing process feel more natural and engaging for students.

Inspired by her methods, I began incorporating more storytelling into my lessons, encouraging my students to write about their lives, dreams, and challenges. I introduced exercises where they could create narratives around personal memories, describe a significant event, or even write about a moment that changed their perspective. This not only helped them develop their writing skills but also allowed them to connect with their peers by sharing their stories. As they listened to each other's experiences, they realized that their voices mattered and that writing was a powerful tool for self-expression.

This approach quickly became one of my students' favorites, as they began to see writing as more than just a classroom task—it became a way for them to express their individuality and creativity. I noticed even my more reluctant writers started participating eagerly, feeling empowered to put their thoughts and emotions into words. As a result, their writing flourished, becoming richer and more expressive, and I witnessed a transformation in their confidence as they discovered the joy of storytelling.

While storytelling unlocked my students' creativity, I knew it was equally important to reinforce the technical aspects of writing. During one of the staff development sessions, I was reintroduced to an old yet powerful technique for teaching writing called dictado, or dictation. This method, once considered outdated, was brought back into focus as a valuable tool for improving students' writing skills. I decided to implement it in my own classroom, using paragraphs from the novel we were reading at the time. This not only reinforced their writing skills but also deepened their comprehension of the text.

By balancing *storytelling* with *dictado*, my students developed both the creative and technical aspects of writing. Their narratives became richer and more expressive, while their sentence structure, punctuation, and attention to detail improved significantly. It was through this combination that I saw the most growth, as students became more confident writers, equipped with both the tools of self-expression and the technical skills to communicate effectively.

When implementing dictado in my classroom, I started by reading the entire paragraph aloud so students could hear it in context. Then, I dictated the paragraph word by word, guiding them on where to insert commas, periods, and other punctuation marks. After dictating, I would read the paragraph a third time, giving students a chance to correct any missed words or punctuation. Once they completed their work, we moved on to peer editing, allowing students to review each other's writing.

As students became more comfortable with the technique, I introduced a collaborative element, pairing them up to dictate the passage to each other.

This peer-to-peer practice not only built their confidence but also strengthened their understanding of proper sentence structure and punctuation, further reinforcing the technical skills they were developing.

One of the most inspiring sessions I attended was with Dr. Stephen Krashen, a renowned expert on language acquisition, who spoke about the natural process of how we learn languages. He emphasized that language acquisition occurs most effectively when learners are exposed to a language-rich environment filled with comprehensible and meaningful input, rather than through forced drills or rote memorization. Dr. Krashen explained that when students are immersed in engaging and authentic language experiences, they absorb the language more naturally, much like how children learn their first language.

One particular strategy he shared left a lasting impression on me: keeping a small comic book in the language you are learning can significantly boost your language acquisition. The visuals, combined with simple yet contextually rich language, make comic books an ideal tool for enhancing vocabulary and comprehension without feeling overwhelming. This idea struck me as both practical and effective, as it aligned perfectly with the concept of making language learning enjoyable and accessible.

Inspired by Dr. Krashen's insight, I began incorporating comic books into my classroom, encouraging my students to explore them as a fun way to improve their reading skills. I noticed that even my more hesitant readers were drawn to the colorful illustrations and engaging storylines, which made them more willing to take risks with their language. As they read the comic books, they began to pick up new vocabulary, understand sentence structures, and develop a deeper appreciation for the language. It was a powerful reminder that language learning doesn't have to be confined to textbooks; it can be both enjoyable and impactful when approached creatively. This simple addition became a favorite activity in my class, and I saw my students' confidence in reading and understanding English grow as they eagerly shared their favorite stories with one another.

Throughout these sessions, one theme remained constant: the importance of viewing ourselves as lifelong learners. Each workshop, seminar, and training reinforced that teaching is an evolving craft that requires us to stay curious, adaptable, and open to new ideas. It wasn't just about accumulating techniques—it was about developing a mindset that welcomed growth and change.

The application of these new, research-based methods always made teaching more enjoyable for me. I found that when I experimented with innovative strategies, my enthusiasm was contagious, and my students became more engaged, eager to participate, and willing to take risks in their learning.

As I returned to my classroom after each session, I felt a renewed sense of purpose. I began to see staff development not as an obligation but as a privilege—an opportunity to refine my skills, connect with other educators, and, most importantly, better serve my students. It wasn't just about learning how to teach; it was about learning how to be the best teacher I could be.

The journey of staff development taught me that true education isn't confined to the walls of a classroom or the pages of a textbook. It's a continuous process of learning, reflecting, and growing. These experiences not only shaped my teaching techniques but also deepened my belief in the transformative power of education. And as I moved forward in my teaching career, I knew that every workshop I attended, every idea I explored, and every strategy I implemented would not only shape me as an educator but would also impact the lives of every student who walked through my door.

In addition to the many staff development sessions that shaped my teaching journey, one that left a lasting impact on my approach to writing instruction was the Abydos Writing Institute. This training provided me with a deeper understanding of how to guide students through the writing process, particularly when it came to English Language Learners (ELs). Abydos emphasized writing as a form of personal expression, and it equipped me with practical tools to help students organize their thoughts and find their voice. I learned strategies for modeling writing techniques, using mentor texts, and encouraging students to reflect on their work. Abydos reinforced my belief that writing is not just about mechanics but about communicating ideas and emotions in a meaningful way.

Teacher Tip

Don't feel like you have to overhaul your teaching all at once. When you attend staff development sessions, pick just one or two ideas that really speak to you—maybe a SIOP strategy or a creative way to spark higher order thinking. Try them out in your classroom and see how your students respond. What worked? What didn't? Teaching is all about experimenting, reflecting, and adjusting. Over time, these small changes can make a big difference—not just in how you teach, but in how your students learn, engage, and grow alongside you.

Parent Tip

Teachers are always learning too, attending workshops and trainings to find better ways to support your child's education. One of the best ways you can help at home is by asking your child's teacher about any new strategies they're using in the classroom. A simple question like, "Is there anything I can do at home to reinforce what they're learning?" can go a long way. When home and school work together, it creates a steady, supportive environment that helps your child thrive.

19 Using Technology to Develop Language Learning

In recent years, I've seen firsthand how technology has quietly reshaped education, not through flashy gimmicks but through meaningful, everyday changes in the classroom. As a teacher, especially one working with ELs, I've come to view technology not as a luxury, but as a lifeline—a bridge that helps my students cross over the difficult terrain of language learning. With tools like iPads, AI-powered programs, and interactive reading platforms, I've been able to tailor my instruction to meet my students exactly where they are, whether they're just beginning to grasp English or pushing forward into more complex texts.

Reading, in particular, has always been a tough mountain to climb for many of my students. The language feels foreign, the vocabulary overwhelming, and the texts can feel like closed doors. To open those doors, I integrated programs like ESL ReadingSmart and 123 Reading into our daily lessons. These tools allowed students to listen to audio versions of stories, practice vocabulary through interactive games, and complete comprehension tasks at their own pace. I remember one student who was initially so shy about reading aloud in class. With time, and a lot of quiet practice using these tools, she began to speak up more, until one day she smiled and read an entire paragraph in front of her classmates. It was a small moment, but it felt huge—for both of us.

One of the most rewarding aspects of using ESL ReadingSmart was the real-time feedback it gave us. The program generated visual charts showing students what skills they had mastered and where they still needed work. For example, it might highlight that a student had a strong grasp of identifying main ideas but needed help with making inferences. I used these visuals during one-on-one conferences, showing each student their progress. These weren't just graphs—they were confidence boosters. I'll never forget the pride on one student's face as she saw how much new vocabulary she had learned. It was like the numbers and visuals gave her permission to believe in herself.

This kind of targeted insight also helped me become a better teacher. I could quickly see who needed support with high-frequency words and who was ready for more advanced fluency work. It allowed me to adapt my instruction—sometimes pulling a student aside for extra help with flashcards, other times celebrating progress with a quick handwritten note or shoutout. These simple acknowledgments often sparked more effort and motivation than any test score ever could.

iPads added another layer of possibility to our classroom. They became powerful tools, not just because they were fun to use, but because they helped my students engage with language through visuals, sound, and movement. Apps like Quizlet turned vocabulary into interactive games, and Seesaw gave students a space to record their thoughts, draw pictures, and express themselves in both English and their home language. One app that stood out was Story Creator—students would record themselves narrating a sequence of images, practicing their pronunciation while building storytelling skills. For many, it was the first time they heard their own voices in English, and that experience alone gave them a sense of ownership over their learning.

Of course, using technology came with its challenges. I quickly learned that having clear expectations was essential. I introduced a "parking" rule—when we weren't using iPads, students had to place them face-down on the "garage" part of their desks. This simple routine kept us focused and preserved the value of the tools for when they were needed the most. What surprised me, though, was how naturally students embraced this structure. They understood that technology wasn't replacing learning—it was enhancing it.

With tools like Nearpod, I was also able to differentiate instruction in real time. During a vocabulary lesson, newcomers could match words to pictures while more advanced students used those same words in full sentences. Everyone was engaged, but in ways that met their individual language levels. Built-in audio and picture supports helped ensure comprehension, especially for those still developing literacy skills in English.

Another favorite of mine was BrainPOP. I introduced it to support content-based reading, and it was a hit. The short, animated videos paired with interactive quizzes and reading tasks made abstract concepts more accessible. Students didn't just watch, but they also engaged, read, wrote, and reflected. For some of my most hesitant readers, BrainPOP became their first positive reading experience in English.

What I've learned from all of this is that when used with intention and care, technology doesn't distance us from our students; rather it brings us closer. It gives students the tools they need to take ownership of their learning journey, and it gives teachers the insight and flexibility to support them in meaningful ways. For many of my ELs, what once felt impossible—reading fluently, expressing ideas confidently, and participating fully—has become possible. And that shift, that quiet transformation, is what makes this work so deeply fulfilling.

One of the most moving moments I experienced came from a quiet student named Emily. She rarely spoke during lessons, not because she didn't care, but because the weight of her limited English made speaking in front of others feel overwhelming. I introduced her to an app called Shadow Puppet, a digital storytelling tool that allowed her to create a narrated slideshow about her family. With each image she selected, she recorded short voice clips—at first hesitantly, but with growing confidence. It was a low-pressure way for her to practice pronunciation, and more importantly, to share something personal and meaningful in her own voice.

What started as a small project blossomed into a breakthrough. That simple activity helped Emily find her footing. Little by little, she began to raise her hand, offer comments, and participate in classroom discussions. The app didn't just improve her speaking skills, but it gave her a sense of agency and belonging. Watching her transformation reminded me of why these tools matter so much. When used with intention, they don't just build academic skills; they help students find their voice.

That experience, among many others, showed me how the structured use of iPads could turn the classroom into a space where ELs felt safe, supported, and empowered. The technology wasn't just an aid, but it was a spark for creativity, collaboration, and confidence. By aligning our use of digital tools with clear routines and research-based strategies, I was able to meet my students' diverse needs and help them move beyond the limits of language barriers. What I saw, time and time again, was that when students feel ownership over their learning journey, remarkable growth follows.

Blogging for Language Growth

One of the most unexpectedly powerful tools I ever introduced into my language classroom was something as simple as a blog. I set up a class blog on Weebly—not as a grand experiment, but just as a quiet space where we could connect, reflect, and write together. Every week, I'd post a photo or a short video along with a thought-provoking question. The prompt might be as simple as "What does courage mean to you?" or "Have you ever felt like the 'new kid'?" Students would respond in writing and then read and comment on at least two of their classmates' posts.

At first, it felt like just another activity. But it quickly grew into something so much more. This small, weekly ritual became a cornerstone of our classroom—not just for building reading and writing skills, but for helping students discover their voices and really see each other. For my ELs, especially those still finding their footing in a new language and culture, the blog became a safe, low-pressure place where they could express their thoughts without fear of being judged. They could write at their own pace, go back and revise, and most importantly, they could be heard.

What made this blog different from traditional writing assignments was the interaction it sparked. Students weren't just writing for me—they were writing for each other. They read each other's stories, agreed, disagreed, asked questions, and offered encouragement. To help ELs participate more confidently, I provided sentence starters like "I agree with you because … " or "That reminded me of … "—gentle scaffolds that helped them begin. But something beautiful happened over time: those starters began to disappear. The students no longer needed them. Their responses became more natural, more thoughtful, more theirs.

Each week, I encouraged them to try something new—to use a transition word they'd just learned, to describe something with a vivid detail, to fix one grammatical mistake they were working on. It wasn't about perfection; it was about growth. I used the blog as an informal assessment tool, giving students feedback on their writing in a way that felt natural and supportive. Rather than handing back essays with red marks, I left personalized comments, guiding them gently toward stronger structure, clearer ideas, or more precise word choices. It allowed me to track their progress week by week, and more importantly, it helped them see that writing is a process, not a performance.

I remember one student who could barely write a few sentences in the beginning. By the end of the semester, she was writing full paragraphs—clear, confident, and deeply reflective. Her blog posts weren't just stronger in language; they had depth, emotion, and voice.

Beyond language development, the blog created a quiet revolution in critical thinking. I asked students not just to comment, but to truly engage—to push the conversation forward, to respectfully challenge ideas or add new perspectives. I was often surprised and moved by the depth of their insights. And for many students who rarely spoke out loud in class, this became their stage—a space where their ideas mattered and were valued.

The multimedia elements helped, too. A powerful image or a short video clip often sparked a flood of ideas, especially for students who needed visual support to process abstract concepts. The blog wasn't just about writing, it was about connecting language to life, making it real, and relevant.

What touched me most was how much the students cared. They looked forward to reading each other's posts. They waited for comments. They cheered each other on. One student once told me it was the first time she felt "like someone listened" to her in school. And even after they moved on from my class, I'd hear from them. "I miss the blog," they'd say. So do I.

In the end, the blog was never just about practicing grammar or building vocabulary. It became a space of reflection, collaboration, and empowerment. A space where students were not only learning a new language, but also learning to trust themselves, take risks, and engage with the world—and with each other—in meaningful, lasting ways.

Digital Storytelling

One of the most meaningful and memorable projects I introduced in my classroom was digital storytelling. It wasn't just about technology; it was about giving students a platform to share a piece of themselves. The idea was simple: use multimedia tools to tell a personal story. But the results were anything but simple. These short videos or narrated slideshows became powerful vehicles for connection, self-expression, and language growth.

We started small. Each student began by brainstorming and writing a script, a process that gently encouraged them to plan, reflect, and think about how to organize their ideas. For many ELs, this was the first time they were asked to tell a story from their own lives in English. It could have been intimidating, but because it was their story, it gave them something to hold onto. Bit by bit, they narrated their scripts, recorded their voices, and brought the stories to life with images, text, and even music. The creativity that poured out of them was incredible.

For my ELs, this project was a game changer. Traditional assignments can often feel restrictive, especially when language is still forming. But digital storytelling offered freedom—it allowed them to express themselves in ways that felt more natural and less pressured. With visuals to support their words and the ability to rehearse and revise their narration, students were able to experiment with new vocabulary, play with sentence structure, and find their rhythm in English. It was multimodal learning at its best—reading, writing, speaking, and listening all rolled into one project, woven through a story that mattered to them.

The moment they shared their stories with the class was something I'll never forget. There was pride in their eyes—many of them had never presented in front of a group before, yet here they were, voices recorded, stories playing on the screen, and their classmates listening intently. The response from peers was always kind, always encouraging. That positive feedback built confidence, and I watched students who were once quiet and hesitant begin to sit a little straighter, speak a little louder, and believe a little more in themselves.

What struck me most was the way these stories brought our classroom community together. Through their digital projects, students shared pieces of their cultures, their families, their challenges, and their dreams. We learned about one another in ways that textbooks could never offer. The classroom slowly became a place where students didn't just learn English—they connected, empathized, and grew together.

Digital storytelling wasn't just a project; it was a celebration of identity and a testament to the idea that language learning doesn't have to be dry or formulaic. With the right tools and the right opportunities, students don't just acquire language—they use it to tell their stories, build bridges, and discover their voice.

Peer Editing with Google Docs

One of the best decisions I made to support my students' writing—and to build a stronger sense of collaboration in the classroom—was to introduce peer editing through Google Docs. What started as a simple way to share drafts quickly turned into a transformative experience that reshaped how students thought about writing. It moved them away from the idea that writing is a one-and-done task, and toward understanding that it's a process—one that grows stronger with feedback, revision, and reflection.

To guide the process and help students focus their attention, I introduced a simple but powerful routine. As they reviewed their peers' drafts, I asked them to give two specific positive comments, highlighting what worked well, and then ask one question about an idea that needed more development. Something like, "Can you explain this part more?" or "What happened next?" This framework gave students just enough structure to feel confident in giving feedback, and it reminded them that revision isn't about criticism—it's about curiosity and clarity.

At first, there was hesitation. Some students weren't used to the idea of sharing their work with a classmate, much less having someone comment on it. But once we eased into the rhythm of giving and receiving feedback, something clicked. They began reading more attentively, thinking about clarity, structure, and even word choice—not just in their peer's work, but in their own. It was incredible to see how offering feedback helped them become more thoughtful writers themselves.

What made this all work so well was the interactive nature of Google Docs. Students could highlight specific sentences, ask questions in the margins, or suggest a new way to phrase an idea—all in real time. The feedback wasn't vague or overwhelming. It was targeted and practical. And because it happened while the writing process was still fresh, students could revise with purpose and confidence. For many, it made editing feel less like a chore and more like an act of collaboration.

One moment that really stayed with me was when a quiet student—someone who rarely raised his hand—left a thoughtful and encouraging comment on a classmate's draft. When the student receiving the feedback read it, his whole face lit up. That simple moment of being seen, of having his effort acknowledged by a peer, carried more weight than any grade or teacher comment could. These moments of connection reminded me that writing, at its core, is about being understood.

What mattered just as much as the technical aspect was the sense of community that grew out of these sessions. As students gave each other suggestions and encouragement, they began to trust one another more. They no longer viewed each other as just classmates but as resources—supporters in a shared journey to improve. For my ELs, this was especially powerful. Reading their peers' work exposed them to new vocabulary and sentence structures, while receiving thoughtful feedback in a safe, structured way helped them take more confident steps forward in their own writing.

In the end, these peer editing sessions weren't just about polishing drafts. They helped students internalize a deeper truth: writing isn't about getting it right the first time—it's about growth, revision, and the courage to keep improving. Using Google Docs didn't just make peer editing easier—it made it more human. It turned writing into something dynamic, collaborative, and deeply personal.

Interactive Quizzes and Polls

At the time, I didn't use Kahoot!, as it wasn't available yet. Instead, I utilized other interactive apps and activities that were popular, including Smartboard-based games and tools like Plickers and ClassTools.net. One of the most engaging activities was a sorting game where students interacted with a line of virtual "clothes" on the Smartboard. The teacher would give verbal instructions, such as, "Pick the red shirt," or "Find the item with the number 5," and students would physically select the correct item from the line. This hands-on, interactive approach encouraged students to follow instructions and reinforced key concepts in a fun, engaging way.

Additionally, Plickers allowed me to conduct live polls and quizzes with instant feedback, making it a great tool for formative assessments. Students answered questions by holding up QR code-style cards, which I could scan with my smartphone to instantly gather responses. This helped me assess their understanding on the spot and adjust instruction as needed.

Similarly, ClassTools.net offered customizable templates for quiz games and interactive activities. One of the most popular features was the Fruit Machine, a randomized quiz generator that turned review sessions into fun, competitive games. These platforms, combined with the Smartboard activities, helped keep students engaged, motivated, and active participants in their learning.

By integrating these tools, I was able to create a classroom atmosphere that felt dynamic and enjoyable while reinforcing learning concepts in a meaningful way.

Language Learning Apps

To help my students keep learning beyond the walls of the classroom, I began introducing them to language learning apps like Duolingo. I wanted them to feel that learning didn't have to stop when the lesson ended—and that they had tools right at their fingertips to continue growing. These apps gave them the freedom to practice vocabulary and grammar at their own pace, whether they were riding the bus home or relaxing in the evening. What I loved most was seeing how students started to take ownership of their learning. Some would excitedly show me their progress streaks or the new words they'd mastered, and it became clear that the combination of structured classroom instruction and independent, app-based practice was helping them gain confidence and momentum. For many of them, this mix of guided and self-directed learning made language acquisition feel more natural, personal, and even fun.

The Rise of Artificial Intelligence in Education

AI represents one of the most significant advancements in education. AI-powered platforms, such as Khanmigo by Khan Academy, adapt to each student's learning style and pace, creating individualized learning pathways. This personalized approach ensures that every student can progress at their own pace, mastering concepts before moving on to more challenging material.

In terms of language learning, AI-powered tools have been transformative. Voice recognition software and AI-driven chatbots allow students to practice speaking and writing with instant feedback. In my classroom, I observed how these AI tools encouraged students to experiment with language, making them more confident in their abilities.

Educational Strategy: Balancing AI with Human Interaction

To maximize AI's benefits without losing the human touch:

1 **Use AI as a Supplement**: AI should enhance, not replace, teacher interaction. Pair AI tools with personalized feedback and group discussions.

2 **Teach Responsible AI Use:** Guide students in understanding the ethical implications of AI and data privacy.

3 **Balance Technology with Human Connection**: Regularly check in with students to provide the empathy and encouragement that technology can't offer.

Finding the Balance Between Technology and Human Interaction

While technology offers incredible benefits in the classroom, it should never replace the human element in teaching. The tools we use, from apps to digital platforms, can enhance the learning experience, but they cannot replicate the empathy, understanding, and personalized attention that a teacher provides. Technology cannot replace the human connection that fosters a sense of belonging, builds trust, and addresses the emotional and social needs of students. As a teacher, I understood that my role wasn't just to deliver content, but to support my students' overall well-being and development. In my classroom, I made it a priority to use technology as a tool to support learning, not as a substitute for the vital teacher–student relationships that are at the heart of education.

The empathy and encouragement I offered created an environment where students felt safe to take risks, make mistakes, and express themselves without fear of judgment. This emotional support is crucial for all students, but it is especially important for language learners, who often face challenges in expressing themselves in a new language. By pairing technology with human interaction, I was able to create a balanced learning experience where students not only advanced in their academic skills but also built the confidence needed to engage in the learning process.

For example, while digital platforms like ESL ReadingSmart and Duolingo helped students work on their language skills independently, I always followed up with one-on-one or small group sessions to provide targeted feedback and encouragement. This combination allowed students to benefit from the self-paced nature of technology while still receiving the personalized attention and emotional support that can only come from a teacher. By taking time to listen to my students' concerns, celebrate their progress, and offer guidance when they faced challenges, I ensured that they felt both challenged and cared for. This balance made their learning journey not only more effective but also more meaningful.

Ultimately, blending technology with personal interaction allowed me to meet students where they were and provide the kind of support that is necessary for their success. While technology helped to engage and empower students, it was the teacher's presence, guidance, and genuine care that truly made a lasting impact. This approach ensured that learning was not just about acquiring skills or knowledge, but also about developing as confident, capable individuals who felt supported throughout their educational journey.

Conclusion

Over the past few years, I've seen how the integration of technology, and more recently, AI, has truly reshaped the way we teach and learn. It's opened up exciting new possibilities, making learning more personal, more interactive, and, in many cases, more engaging. Tools like AI-powered writing assistants, adaptive learning platforms, and real-time feedback systems have given us the ability to better understand where each student is and what they need. For language learners in particular, these tools can be game changers. With digital flashcards, interactive reading programs, and even speech recognition software, students can practice at their own pace, revisit difficult concepts, and build confidence bit by bit—all without fear of judgment or pressure.

But as helpful and innovative as these tools are, I've found myself returning to the same truth again and again: no piece of technology can replace the human connection between teacher and student. It's that connection—built on empathy, encouragement, and understanding—that truly makes a difference. Yes, AI can help correct a sentence or suggest a better word, but it can't celebrate a student's small victory the way a teacher can. It can't sense when a learner needs a gentle push or a moment of grace. And it certainly can't replace the trust that grows when a student knows someone genuinely believes in them.

That's why, as we embrace these new tools, we have to do so thoughtfully. Technology should support our work, not define it. When used well, it can create more room for teachers to focus on what matters most: connecting with students, guiding them, and helping them grow not just academically, but emotionally and socially too.

The key, I believe, is balance. When we combine the power of technology with the warmth of human connection, we create something truly special—classrooms where every student feels seen, supported, and empowered. And as we prepare students for a world that's changing faster than ever, that balance will be more important than ever. Because while the tools may evolve, the heart of teaching remains the same: helping students find their voice, believe in their potential, and step into the future with confidence.

Teacher Tip

In today's classroom, I've found that technology, when used with purpose, can be one of our greatest allies in supporting language learners. It's not just about adding gadgets or apps—it's about opening doors. With the right digital tools and resources, we can create lessons that feel more interactive, more personalized, and far more engaging than traditional methods alone.

What I love about using technology is how it allows students to learn in ways that work best for them. Some might thrive using apps like Duolingo or Quizlet to build their vocabulary through repetition and play. Others come alive when given a chance to record their voices and share their thoughts using platforms like Flipgrid, where speaking and listening practice feels safe, supported, and even fun. Multimedia resources—videos, audio clips, and interactive websites—also go a long way in helping students make sense of language, especially for those who struggle with traditional text-based materials. Seeing and hearing the content often makes it click in a way that reading alone sometimes doesn't.

But it's not just about language. When we integrate technology into learning, we're also helping students build digital skills they'll carry into the future. Navigating apps, recording audio, typing responses—these are the tools of today's world. By encouraging the students to engage with technology meaningfully, we're giving them more than just academic support—we're giving them confidence, agency, and a sense of ownership over their learning.

What's been most rewarding for me is watching students start to take initiative—practicing on their own, exploring new resources, even teaching each other how to use a tool I introduced. When they see learning as something they can shape themselves, that's when real growth happens. And technology, when used thoughtfully, helps make that possible.

Parent Tip

Parents play such an important role in helping children grow as language learners, especially when it comes to using technology at home. One of the things I found especially helpful was encouraging parents to make these learning tools part of their child's daily routine—not in a strict or overwhelming way, but more like creating a fun, regular habit. For example, I often encouraged parents to check in by asking, "What level have you reached on ESL ReadingSmart this week?" That one simple question often led to smiles, a sense of pride, and sometimes even a little friendly competition among siblings.

It also helped to give parents a clear, manageable time frame. Just 15 to 20 minutes a day on an app like ESL ReadingSmart can make a real difference. These programs are designed to be engaging and interactive, so students often enjoy them without even realizing they're learning. I reminded parents that even if it looks like their child is just playing a game or watching a video, they're actually building vocabulary, grammar skills, and confidence—all while having fun.

Of course, every home situation is different. I remember one student telling me that he couldn't use the program at home because his parents didn't allow him on the computer after school. That moment stuck with me—it reminded me how vital communication with families is. When teachers and parents work together and understand each other's perspectives, it becomes much easier to find creative solutions. Even a quick note or casual conversation can help parents see the value in these tools and how they fit into their child's learning journey.

That's why I always encouraged parents to sit with their child once in a while, explore the platform together, and talk about what they're learning. It not only makes the child feel supported but also helps the parent understand just how much language development is happening through these tools.

At the same time, it's important to guide children toward quality content and be mindful of screen time. With so many distractions online, it helps when parents steer their children toward resources that truly support language growth. Even brief, consistent involvement—like checking in, offering encouragement, or celebrating progress—can make a meaningful impact.

By staying engaged in small, intentional ways, parents help their children build not only language skills but also confidence, independence, and digital literacy. And in my experience, those little moments—asking about a level, cheering on a new word learned, sharing a quick high-five—often become the most memorable steps on a child's path to success.

20 Co-teaching

"It's like riding a tandem bicycle—you have to adapt to the pace of the other rider." That's how Mrs. J, an ELA teacher I had the privilege of co-teaching with, once described our experience. The image stuck with me because it perfectly captures what co-teaching is all about: balance, coordination, and trust. You can't pedal too fast or too slow, you have to find a shared rhythm, communicate constantly, and keep your eyes on the same goal: helping students grow.

Co-teaching is more than simply sharing a classroom; it's about building a true partnership grounded in mutual respect and a shared commitment to students. In our case, we co-taught a class that included several ELs. Together, Mrs. J and I combined our strengths, her expertise in literature and writing and my background in language development, to ensure all students had access to rich, meaningful instruction. These kinds of partnerships are where I've seen some of the most powerful teaching and learning happen.

One of the greatest rewards of co-teaching has been the chance to work alongside passionate, dedicated professionals like Mrs. J, who brings fresh perspectives and new strategies into the classroom. Whether it's through creative lesson design, strong classroom management, or deep content knowledge, each co-teacher I've worked with has helped me become a better educator. In our ELA class, we designed lessons that engaged students at all levels, using scaffolds, visuals, and vocabulary support to make complex texts more accessible without watering down the content.

Of course, co-teaching isn't always seamless. In the early stages of working together, it's normal to encounter moments of miscommunication or differences in teaching styles. Mrs. J and I had to navigate these early on, figuring out when to lead, when to support, and how to divide responsibilities in a way that felt balanced. What made it work was our willingness to talk honestly, reflect together, and always keep students at the center of our decisions. Those conversations helped us build trust and ultimately brought us closer as colleagues.

Perhaps the most important lesson I've learned through co-teaching is the power of partnership. When two educators work side by side—especially in a class with diverse learning needs—they not only share the workload, but also the victories. The students notice, too. They see their teachers modeling collaboration, respect, and a shared purpose. That example becomes part of the classroom culture. It shows them that learning is a team effort and that every voice, teacher and student alike, matters.

Co-teaching with Mrs. J and others has taught me that when we work together with openness and purpose, the classroom becomes a space where both teachers and students thrive.

Collaborative Planning: The Foundation of Successful Co-teaching

Co-teaching doesn't really start at the classroom door; it starts at the planning table. One of the most essential elements of a successful co-teaching experience is what happens behind the scenes: those planning sessions where two educators come together not just to organize a lesson, but to align their thinking, share their ideas, and truly collaborate.

I've learned that when co-teachers take the time to plan intentionally, the difference is felt in the classroom. Students notice when teachers are in sync. There's a natural flow, a shared rhythm, and a clarity in the instruction that doesn't happen by accident, but it comes from thoughtful preparation.

I still remember one partnership where my co-teacher and I spent hours carefully designing lessons that addressed both content and language development. We knew our students came from different linguistic and academic backgrounds, so we made it a point to map out clear content objectives while embedding language support at every step. Those sessions were filled with back-and-forth questions, lightbulb moments, and even the occasional laughter when a creative idea came together.

In another collaboration, I worked with a science teacher who was passionate about her subject but hadn't worked closely with ELs before. During one planning session, we realized that many of our EL students were getting stuck, not on the science concepts themselves, but on the language used to explain them. So, we tried something new: before diving into the lesson, I introduced key vocabulary using visuals, gestures, and real-life examples. Then she stepped in to connect those words to the core scientific ideas. It was a simple shift, but it made a huge difference. Our students became more engaged and confident because we had cleared a path for them to access the content.

What I've come to understand is that collaborative planning isn't about dividing tasks down the middle, it's about bringing two sets of strengths together and finding ways to weave them into one strong, cohesive lesson. When both teachers have a voice in the planning process, it leads to a more inclusive, intentional, and responsive classroom experience for all learners.

The Role of Trust and Flexibility in Co-teaching

If there's one lesson co-teaching has taught me over the years, it's this: trust and flexibility aren't optional, they're essential. A successful co-teaching relationship rests on the foundation of mutual respect, openness, and a shared willingness to adapt. When those pieces fall into place, something powerful happens, two teachers with different styles, backgrounds, and strengths come together to create a richer, more responsive classroom experience for every student.

Co-teaching is more than just standing at the front of a classroom together. It's about recognizing that there's no single "right" way to teach, and being willing to let go of personal preferences in favor of a greater goal: student progress. That kind of partnership takes humility. It takes give and take. And it takes trust.

I'll be honest, there were times in my own co-teaching journey when I found it difficult to step back and let my co-teacher take the lead, especially when their approach was very different from mine. At first, I worried what if it didn't work? What if students didn't connect? But over time, I began to see that trusting my co-teacher didn't mean giving up on what I believed in; it meant making room for both of our strengths to shine. When we honored each other's contributions, we created something stronger together than we ever could have apart.

One experience that really stands out was when I worked with a co-teacher who preferred to stick closely to the textbook. Her lessons were structured and consistent, but I worried that some of our ELs were getting left behind, not because they didn't understand the content, but because the language barrier made the material harder to access. I knew that pushing for big changes too quickly might lead to tension or resistance, so I tried a different approach. I began to gently model strategies, adding visuals, using real-world examples, and introducing hands-on activities that supported language development.

I still remember one lesson where an ELA teacher led a close reading of a poem from the textbook. While she focused on the literary analysis, I quietly passed out a graphic organizer that helped students unpack the imagery and symbolism in a more visual way. At first, I wasn't sure what she'd think. But when she saw how much more engaged the students were, especially those who usually struggled, something shifted. She became curious. She started asking questions. And little by little, she began incorporating similar strategies into her own teaching.

What happened next was something I'll never forget. We began blending our style, her structure and pacing, my creativity and scaffolds, into lessons that truly worked for everyone. Our students responded, and our partnership deepened. We weren't just co-teaching anymore; we were co-learning, co-growing.

That experience reminded me that co-teaching is not about one person giving in or winning over the other. It's about finding common ground, building trust, and being patient enough to let growth unfold naturally. When teachers work together with openness and respect, the classroom becomes more than a place of instruction, it becomes a place where collaboration comes to life and everyone benefits.

The Impact of Co-teaching on Student Learning

There's something special that happens when two teachers come together with a shared purpose, especially in classrooms filled with students who bring diverse backgrounds, learning needs, and language levels. Co-teaching has the power to transform not just how lessons are delivered, but how students experience learning.

For ELs in particular, co-teaching can be a game changer. With two educators in the room, students benefit from more individualized attention, more ways to access the content, and a richer mix of teaching styles. It's like giving students two lenses to view the same material, each one bringing something unique and supportive.

I still remember a literature unit we co-taught that really brought this to life. My ELA co-teacher focused on helping students explore literary elements like theme, tone, and symbolism. Meanwhile, I was right there beside her, breaking down complex language structures, scaffolding vocabulary, and guiding our ELs through unfamiliar grammar. Together, we built a lesson that wasn't just about analyzing a text; it was about making the language of that text accessible and meaningful to every learner in the room.

One of my favorite memories from that unit was a punctuation lesson we turned into a full-body, hands-on experience. We split the class into small groups and handed out strips of paper, each with a sentence written on it. Students had to choose which part of the sentence they wanted to "be" and act it out in front of the class. I remember one student proudly stepping forward as the word "David," using a dramatic gesture to signal the capital letter at the start. Another student wiggled and bounced to show off their action verb. When it came time for the comma, one particularly theatrical student made a sweeping half-circle motion with her foot to represent the pause.

It was fun. It was noisy. And it worked. My co-teacher and I shared the lead seamlessly, while I guided the group discussions and helped students choose their parts she reinforced the punctuation rules and made sure the learning stayed on track. The classroom buzzed with laughter and energy, and even our most reluctant writers were leaning in, fully engaged.

I'll never forget what one student said as we wrapped up: "I never knew punctuation could be fun." That moment reminded me why we do what we do. When we bring energy, movement, and a spirit of collaboration into our teaching, students respond in the most incredible ways. By the end of that lesson, kids who had once stumbled through punctuation exercises were confidently applying the rules in their own writing, with a smile.

Another moment that still sticks with me was during a lesson on figurative language. One student, in particular, struggled deeply with metaphors. She'd often shut down during those discussions, frustrated and convinced she just couldn't "get it." But in our co-teaching setup, while my co-teacher led the main discussion with the class, I was able to sit beside her quietly and walk her through examples, one at a time. I used visuals and simple comparisons to help the ideas click. That one-on-one support, given right in the flow of the lesson, made all the difference. By the end of the unit, she wasn't just understanding metaphors, she was writing her own, and proud of it.

These moments are why I believe so deeply in co-teaching. It's not about two people splitting a classroom—it's about two people coming together to meet students where they are. It's about listening, adapting, and showing students that there's more than one way to learn, and more than one person who believes in their ability to succeed.

Co-teaching reminds me every day that the best classrooms are built on collaboration. And when teachers lift each other up, students rise too.

Finding Our Rhythm: The Learning Curve of Co-teaching

Co-teaching, like any real partnership, comes with its fair share of growing pains. It asks both teachers to show up with open minds, clear communication, and a willingness to adapt. I'll never forget what a seasoned ELA teacher once told me during one of our early planning sessions: "Co-teaching is like riding a tandem bicycle, you have to find a shared rhythm, adjust your pace, and trust the other rider." That image stayed with me, because it captures the essence of what makes co-teaching work: balance, coordination, and trust.

When one teacher speeds ahead or holds back, things get wobbly. But when both find a rhythm together, when they listen, adjust, and move with purpose, the ride becomes not only smoother but genuinely rewarding.

One of the most meaningful (and admittedly challenging) co-teaching experiences I had was with a teacher who favored traditional, lecture-based instruction. Her lessons were well-structured and thorough, but I noticed that some of our ELs were quietly slipping through the cracks. They struggled to stay engaged, not because they lacked ability, but because the language and delivery didn't always meet them where they were.

At first, I wasn't sure how to introduce a more interactive approach without disrupting her flow or stepping on her toes. I knew that pushing for immediate change wouldn't help our partnership, or our students. So instead, I took a quieter path: I started modeling.

During one lesson on literary themes, she led the class through a detailed analysis. While she guided the discussion, I gathered a small group of students and introduced a vocabulary-building activity tied to the text. We used visuals, real-world examples, and word maps to break things down. I didn't say much, just let the learning speak for itself.

To her credit, my co-teacher noticed. She saw how the students, especially our ELs, lit up with understanding. They were more engaged, more confident, and more willing to take academic risks. Slowly, she began to experiment— adding a visual here, tweaking a question there, and over time, our styles began to blend. We didn't just take turns teaching; we started to teach together.

There's one student I'll always remember from that class. At the beginning of the year, he rarely raised his hand. He seemed unsure of himself, especially when it came to reading and participating in group work. But with the layered support we built into our co-taught lessons, he began to thrive. He not only joined in discussions, he started to lead them. By the end of the unit, his reading comprehension had improved significantly, and so had his confidence. That transformation wasn't just a win for him, it was a reminder of why co-teaching, when done with trust and intention, can be so powerful.

Co-teaching doesn't mean one teacher changing for the other; it means finding a shared path, one that honors both styles and puts students first. Like that tandem bicycle, it takes effort to find the right balance. But once you do, the journey becomes smoother, more connected, and undeniably more joyful—for teachers and students alike.

Overcoming the challenges of co-teaching begins with one simple but powerful act: open communication. Talk honestly about your differences in teaching styles, share your goals, and find common ground through respectful dialogue. In my experience, leading by example, quietly modeling strategies that support student engagement, often builds trust more effectively than words alone. Flexibility is also key; sometimes it means adjusting your style to align with your partner's and other times it means trying something new for the sake of your students. For those new to co-teaching, my biggest advice is this: prioritize communication, embrace each other's strengths, and be willing to adapt. Reflect often on what's working and what needs adjusting, it's in those moments of reflection that real growth happens. And don't forget to celebrate the wins, big or small. Whether it's a student finally grasping a tough concept or a lesson that flowed beautifully between the two of you, those shared successes are the heartbeat of a strong co-teaching partnership.

Co-teaching has not only enriched my students' learning experiences but has also transformed my own understanding of teaching as a collaborative and ever-evolving practice. It has shown me the power of partnership in education, how two minds working together can create a classroom environment far more dynamic and inclusive than one teacher could achieve alone. Through co-teaching, I have learned that collaboration is not just about dividing responsibilities; it is about embracing the unique strengths, perspectives, and teaching styles of your partner to build something greater than the sum of its parts.

One of the most valuable lessons I have gained is the importance of creating a space where every student feels seen, heard, and supported. This means tailoring our approaches to meet the diverse needs of learners— whether through differentiated instruction, scaffolded support, or innovative activities that engage students on multiple levels. Co-teaching has allowed me to see firsthand how combining expertise can lead to more personalized learning experiences. For instance, while one teacher might focus on academic rigor, the other might emphasize relational connections, creating a balance that nurtures both the mind and the heart of each student.

Moreover, co-teaching has reinforced the idea that education is a shared journey, not just for students but also for teachers. It has taught me to approach challenges with an open mind, to listen actively to my co-teacher's perspectives, and to view differing opinions as opportunities for growth. By embracing the strengths of my co-teaching partners, I have witnessed how mutual respect and adaptability can foster an environment that empowers every learner to reach their full potential. This experience has not only made me a better teacher but has also deepened my appreciation for the collaborative nature of education and the profound impact it can have on students' lives.

Teacher Tip

At its core, co-teaching is all about partnership, and like any good partnership, it thrives on clear communication, thoughtful planning, and a shared commitment to working together. One of the first and most important steps is to establish roles and responsibilities early on. It may sound simple, but setting those expectations upfront can prevent confusion and help both teachers focus on what they do best. Whether one of you takes the lead during a particular lesson while the other offers support, or you co-deliver the content side by side, knowing who's doing what makes everything run more smoothly and allows each teacher's strengths to shine.

Planning together is another cornerstone of successful co-teaching. When both teachers are involved in lesson design, you're not just dividing the work, you're blending ideas, experiences, and talents to create something more powerful than either of you could do alone. I've worked with co-teachers who were incredible at breaking down complex grammar and others who could lead literary discussions that made students genuinely excited about a poem or short story. When we brought those skills together, the lessons came alive, and our students benefited from the richness of both perspectives.

One of the things I love most about co-teaching is how flexible it allows instruction to be. With two educators in the room, you can move easily between whole-group teaching, small-group activities, and one-on-one support—all within the same lesson. If one student needs extra help understanding a concept, one of us can step in without disrupting the flow of the class. If a group needs extension work, we're ready. That real-time responsiveness is one of the greatest gifts co-teaching offers.

In the end, the most successful co-teaching partnerships are built on mutual respect, open communication, and the willingness to learn from one another. When both teachers bring their full selves to the classroom and work toward a shared vision, the result is a learning environment where students feel seen, supported, and truly inspired to grow.

Parent Tip

If your child has more than one teacher working with them in the same classroom, you're seeing co-teaching in action. This is a collaborative teaching approach where two educators team up to support all students, and it can be especially helpful for children who are learning English or need a little extra guidance. Co-teaching allows each teacher to bring their strengths to the table: one might focus on helping students build language skills, while the other leads the subject content. Together, they create a more personalized, engaging learning experience that gives your child the support they need to succeed.

You're always welcome to reach out to either teacher if you have questions or concerns about how your child is doing. Both teachers work closely to support your child and can offer insights into the strategies being used in class. By keeping in touch with them, you'll get a clearer picture of your child's progress, any areas they might be finding challenging, and simple ways to help at home. For example, the teachers might suggest vocabulary games, reading strategies, or fun activities you can do together to reinforce what they're learning.

At its heart, co-teaching is not just a partnership between two teachers; it's a partnership with you, too. Your involvement makes a real difference. When families and teachers work together, we build a strong circle of support around your child, helping them feel confident, encouraged, and ready to thrive both in and out of the classroom.

21 Data-driven Teaching

Data-driven instruction has reshaped the way we teach. It's no longer just about following instincts, but about using meaningful insights to guide each student's journey. Over time, I've developed simple but powerful systems to track student progress, including personalized spreadsheets and portfolios. These tools don't just help me as a teacher—they help students see their growth with their own eyes. By building in moments for students to reflect on their goals and milestones, I've seen a genuine shift in how they view themselves as learners. They begin to take ownership, and with that come pride, accountability, and motivation.

One student stands out in my memory. He had grown increasingly discouraged by low grades, beginning to link his academic struggles to his self-worth. I could see how deflated he felt. One day, I sat down with him and opened his ESL folder. We flipped back to his very first writing samples—sentences filled with hesitations, fragments, and errors. Then we looked at his most recent work: clear, confident paragraphs with improved grammar and expanded vocabulary. His eyes lit up. "I wrote that?" he asked in disbelief. That small moment became a turning point. Instead of chasing perfection, he began to focus on progress. And with that mindset shift came new energy, a willingness to try again, and a deeper belief in himself.

Stories like his remind me why tracking progress matters so much. Yes, I use spreadsheets and folders, but they're not just about numbers. They're about creating tools that help both the teacher and the student believe in growth.

Technology has made this process even more powerful. Programs like ESL ReadingSmart provide visual tools, charts, graphs, color-coded reports, that make student growth easier to interpret and share. These visuals help teachers see patterns quickly, but more importantly, they help students see their own potential. I often share these charts in one-on-one conferences. The smiles I see when a student realizes how much they've improved? Priceless. It boosts confidence, helps them tackle bigger challenges, and makes learning feel like something they own.

One of the most helpful tools I used was a custom spreadsheet (see Figure 21.1) where I tracked each student's performance across different benchmarks, from classroom assessments to standardized tests like TELPAS, OLPT, and DRA2.

I used visual codes to highlight student needs, light shading for students ready to exit ESL, medium shading for those needing continued monitoring, and a darker shade for unique cases. For instance, Lesly was a newcomer who made incredible progress in her first year. She met all the criteria to exit the program, but I shaded her row differently to signal to future teachers that she might still need cultural and linguistic support. That small formatting choice ensured she wasn't overlooked or expected to navigate everything on her own.

This kind of nuance is what makes data powerful. It doesn't have to reduce students to numbers. Used thoughtfully, it can tell a story and guide decisions that are full of empathy.

These moments reaffirm that reteaching isn't a step backward. It's a chance to slow down, to meet students where they are, and to help them build stronger foundations. With the help of shared data, we could adjust instruction in real time, not months later.

Even the color-coded spreadsheet helped guide these conversations. When I'd meet with students individually, I'd point to their yellow or green highlights

Grade	DRA2 Scores		TELPAS scores /2009 Composit Rating	OLPT Scores/ 2009	Reading TAKS 2009	DA Writing scores 2009	Teacher-student observation	TELPAS Writing Scores
	Text Level	Fiction/Non-fiction						
6	50	F	Int	C/LES	F	1	INT	AH
6	40	N	ADV	F/FES	P	1	ADV	AH
6	24	F	INT	E/FES	F	0	INT	ADV
6	40	F	ADV	E/FES	F	2	ADV	INT
6	40	F	ADV	F/FES	P	2	ADV	AH
6	40	N	AH	F/FES	P	2	ADV	AH
6	38	N	ADV	C/LES	F	2	ADV	AH
6	40	F	AH	F/FES	P	2	ADV	AH
6	30	F	AH	F/FES	P	2	ADV	AH
6	40	F	AH	F/FES	P	2	ADV	AH
6	40	F	AH	F/FES	P	2	ADV	AH
6	40	F	AH	F/FES	P	3	ADV	AH

Figure 21.1 ESL Progress Tracking Spreadsheet. Shading highlights students' support levels: light for exit ready, medium for ongoing support, and dark for special considerations, ensuring data-driven, empathetic decisions. © Nesreen El-Baz.

and ask: "What are you proud of? What would you like to focus on next?" These weren't just academic check-ins. They were reflective, personal moments where students saw themselves as learners in charge of their journey.

At the end of each student's folder, I included a simple reflection sheet where they could record their monthly grades, track their progress, or occasional setbacks, and write a short reflection. This wasn't just about numbers; it was about helping them pause, look back, and look forward. Some students used it to celebrate growth, others to set new goals, and some to express frustration or recommit to trying harder.

One student once wrote, "I didn't think I was good at reading, but now I can answer harder questions and help my friend. I'm proud of myself."

Over time, these monthly reflections became a space for honest self-assessment and personal growth. Students began to recognize that learning is a journey with ups and downs, and that they were the ones steering it.

Keeping all student data in one clear, organized system helped me move from just managing information to truly using it—to personalize instruction, celebrate progress, and support every learner in a meaningful way. With the help of simple tools like Excel, collaborative teamwork, and a bit of creativity, my classroom gradually became a space where growth was not only measured but seen and felt by students. And what's more, this didn't require expensive programs or advanced tech skills. Just thoughtful routines, intentional tracking, and a commitment to making sure no student was invisible.

When I first started implementing data-driven instruction, I quickly learned that the biggest challenge wasn't collecting the data but rather finding the time to use it well. Between lesson planning, grading, and the daily rhythm of teaching, keeping up with my spreadsheets often felt like an extra mountain to climb. There were days I'd glance at my notes and think, I'll update it tomorrow. But eventually, I realized that if I didn't make space for it in my weekly routine, it would never feel manageable. So, I began carving out small, consistent blocks of time either right after major assessments or during Friday planning—to update, reflect, and adjust.

But time wasn't the only hurdle. I also found myself overwhelmed by the sheer volume of information available, reading levels, writing samples, standardized scores, and observational notes. At first, I tried to track everything, and it left me more confused than empowered. It wasn't until I gave myself permission to focus on a few key indicators, like reading comprehension growth or writing fluency that I started to see the patterns that actually mattered. Letting go of the rest was freeing.

Tracking consistency also became a challenge, especially in large ESL classes where student needs vary so widely. I wanted every student's progress to be monitored fairly and regularly, but with so many different levels and starting points, it felt daunting. That's where technology helped. Tools like ESL ReadingSmart and my customized Excel templates made the process more systematic. I could scan through color-coded data and immediately spot who needed extra support and who was ready for the next challenge.

Still, the best breakthroughs came when I wasn't working alone. Collaborating with colleagues made all the difference. I remember one meeting where we sat around the table, each with our data in hand, looking at results from a recent reading assessment. We divided the tasks; one teacher focused on comprehension scores, another on vocabulary, a third on writing, and then shared our insights. The conversation was energizing. We left with lesson plans that were sharper and more targeted than anything we could have created alone.

One strategy that helped me stay grounded was building data check-ins into my schedule. After every unit, I set aside time to update my tracker and reflect on what the numbers were really saying. At semester's end, I used the full picture to plan interventions, set new goals, and highlight wins—both big and small. Yes, it took discipline to build the habit, but once it became part of my teaching rhythm, the system felt like an extension of my practice rather than an extra burden.

And I always reminded myself: this wasn't about chasing perfection. It was about using tools that helped me see my students more clearly, recognize their progress, and respond with purpose.

If you're just starting out with data-driven teaching, don't feel like you need to do it all at once. Pick one or two things to track, maybe it's reading fluency, or writing growth—and commit to checking in regularly. Over time, you'll build a system that works for you, one that makes your teaching more intentional and helps your students see just how far they've come.

Because in the end, data isn't just numbers on a page, it's a mirror that reflects growth, effort, and potential. And when used with care, it becomes one of the most powerful tools we have to support every learner's path to success.

Teacher Tip

If you're thinking about bringing data-driven instruction into your classroom, my advice is simple: start small. Pick just one area to focus on, maybe it's tracking your students' writing growth or keeping an eye on their reading comprehension. Begin with tools you already feel comfortable using, like a basic spreadsheet or a simple app, and build from there. You don't need to track everything all at once. What matters most is finding insights you can actually use—those little patterns that help you adjust your teaching in meaningful ways.

Set aside a regular time to reflect, even if it's just fifteen minutes at the end of the week. And don't be afraid to ask a colleague, "What's working for you?" Some of the best strategies I've used came from casual conversations with other teachers. Remember, collecting data isn't the goal, supporting your students is. Let the data be a tool, not a task, and allow it to guide you toward what really matters: helping every learner move forward.

Parent Tip

Stay connected to your child's learning by checking in with their teachers—not just about grades, but about the little wins and areas where they're growing. Celebrate those milestones, even the small ones, a new word they've learned, a paragraph they're proud of, or a challenge they've overcome. These moments matter more than we often realize.

At home, try to create a calm space where your child can focus, maybe it's a quiet corner for reading or a few minutes a day to write together. Most importantly, remind them (and yourself) that learning doesn't have to be perfect. It's okay to make mistakes. Progress takes time, and every step forward, no matter how small, is worth celebrating. You're helping them build confidence, not just skills.

Part 6
Conclusion and Resources

22 Full Circle: My Journey of Growth

One day, years after I had moved away from Houston, my phone buzzed with a message notification from a former student, let's call her Gisselle. Her name immediately brought back memories of a bright, determined girl who once sat quietly in my classroom, working hard to decode a language that felt foreign and overwhelming.

Her message read:

> *I always remember you! They asked us to make a speech about a life-changing event, and I wrote about when I walked into your class and had to learn a different language. You were part of that speech.*

She went on to share that she had recently earned her pharmacy technician license and was now preparing to go back to school to pursue an engineering degree. I sat with her words for a long moment, letting them wash over me. That message, so unexpected and sincere, became one of those rare and quiet affirmations that seem to arrive just when you need them the most.

As I reread her words, memories flickered through my mind: afternoons spent tutoring, patiently explaining irregular verbs, celebrating small victories like a perfectly formed sentence or a moment of understanding that lit up her face. I had often wondered whether those moments truly made a difference. And here, in this message, was my answer.

This, I realized, is the quiet miracle of teaching. The moments that feel routine or invisible at the time can ripple outward into a student's life, shaping their confidence and their sense of what is possible. To know that I had played even a small part in her journey was deeply humbling. It reminded me that our work as educators often bears fruit long after our students have left our classrooms. It reminded me that teaching is not only about standards or content—it is about showing up, seeing each student fully, and believing in them until they can believe in themselves.

Gisselle's message was a powerful reminder of the quiet often unseen impact teachers make. Yet there are also moments when that impact is recognized in more visible and public ways, arriving unexpectedly and affirming the work we pour into our students every day.

One afternoon, I received an unexpected email from the district announcing that three ESL teachers had been selected as finalists for the HAABE Houston Teacher of the Year award. To my amazement, my name was among them. I paused and reread the message. Could this be real? A quiet wave of disbelief gave way to a deep, humbling sense of pride. After years of dedication, this recognition felt like a moment of affirmation.

The application required several components, including a recommendation letter from a colleague. Without hesitation, I turned to Ms. H., a seasoned educator whose insight and encouragement had long inspired me. When I asked her, she readily agreed. The very next day, she placed a sealed envelope on my desk.

As I unfolded the letter and began to read her words, I felt a swell of emotion rise within me. She wrote of my great compassion for teaching and my ability to connect with students across backgrounds and academic levels. She spoke of my eagerness to attend professional development workshops and my habit of returning with fresh ideas to share with our team. She described my classroom as a space where students were not only challenged but deeply supported, a place where they were empowered to reach heights they never imagined.

"Her enthusiasm for teaching English Language Learners is infectious," she concluded. "She is a truly exceptional educator."

Reading her letter, I was deeply moved. It was not just her generous words that stayed with me, but the recognition from someone I so deeply admired. It was as though she held up a mirror and reflected back all the moments I had quietly poured into my work, the planning, the encouraging, the striving—and said, I see you. That letter became more than an endorsement.

It was a milestone in my journey, a reminder that even in a profession where so much effort goes unseen, someone had noticed.

I still hold on to that letter. It remains a cherished reminder of the importance of seeing and acknowledging the dedication of those around us. In the flurry of a teacher's day, moving from one lesson to the next, meeting needs, solving problems, we often overlook the quiet heroism of our colleagues. Rarely do we pause to say, "You are doing something remarkable." Ms. H's letter reminded me of how powerful that kind of acknowledgment can be.

Both Ms. H's letter and Gisselle's heartfelt message served as vivid reminders of why I chose this path. They reinforced my belief that teaching is ultimately a journey of human connection. Our efforts may not always be measured in test scores or official outcomes, but they are felt deeply, personally, and often in ways that ripple across a lifetime. Teaching is not only about shaping academic growth; it is about nurturing lives, one interaction, one student at a time.

As educators, we often move through our days with our focus on the next challenge, the next struggling student, the next stack of papers to grade. Rarely do we step back to consider how our work is perceived by others or how it shapes us over time. Ms. H's letter helped me do just that. It validated my efforts, but more than that, it reminded me of the vital importance of honoring the colleagues we walk alongside. Teaching is rarely a solitary pursuit. It is a shared mission, a web of support and collaboration where every gesture of kindness, feedback, or encouragement matters.

It is this dual connection with students and with colleagues that ultimately shaped my growth not only as a teacher but as a parent. Teaching gave me lessons I never expected, lessons that extended well beyond the classroom.

The patience I learned guiding students through the frustrations of mastering a new language became the patience I brought to conversations with my sons. The empathy I practiced while supporting students through their academic and emotional challenges became the foundation for understanding my own children as they navigated their growing worlds. The joy I felt witnessing my students discover their voices mirrored the quiet pride I experienced watching my sons grow into independent, thoughtful young men.

The classroom shaped me in ways I could not have foreseen. Teaching refined how I communicated, how I listened, and how I responded, not just to students, but to those I loved most. It gave me the tools to meet others where they were, to celebrate progress over perfection, and to hold space for growth, even when the path was slow and uncertain.

This transformation was not immediate. It unfolded gradually through years of interactions with students, parents, and fellow educators. Each moment, every breakthrough and challenge, offered a new insight about people and the power of connection. I came to realize that the very skills I had honed while helping a student find their voice, while offering guidance without judgment, and while encouraging perseverance in the face of setbacks were the same skills that had become central to how I parented.

I began to see potential where others might see limitations. I learned to focus on the small, hard-earned victories. I came to understand that real growth rarely arrives in bold declarations but more often in quiet moments of courage and consistency.

This transformation did not happen overnight. It was shaped by countless interactions—with students, their families, and fellow educators. Each conversation, challenge, and breakthrough became a lesson in human connection. I came to understand that the skills I practiced daily in the classroom, helping a struggling learner find their voice, offering feedback that encouraged rather than discouraged, and guiding students through setbacks with compassion, were the very same skills that deepened the bonds I shared with my sons.

I also came to see how these experiences reshaped my view of education itself. When we first moved to Houston, I felt a pang of disappointment when my sons did not pass the entrance exams for a British school. At the time, it felt like a setback and filled me with uncertainty about their academic future. But as I immersed myself in the American education system, through my work and through their experiences, my perspective began to shift. What once seemed like a detour became a discovery.

The American system revealed its strengths in ways I hadn't anticipated. It encouraged my sons to think strategically and creatively, to ask questions, and to approach learning as an exploratory process rather than a rigid formula. I saw how their teachers fostered their independence and critical thinking, empowering them to take ownership of their education. What struck me most was the system's ability to nurture individuality and creativity while still teaching essential skills. My sons were not just learning for tests, but they were developing the tools they needed to navigate a complex world with confidence and curiosity.

Now, looking back, I am deeply grateful for the opportunities this system provided. What initially felt like a failure turned out to be one of the greatest blessings of our journey. My sons grew into independent thinkers who were unafraid to express themselves and tackle challenges with innovation and resilience. They weren't bound by rigid structures or confined to a single way of thinking, they were free to explore, adapt, and grow into individuals ready to face a world of possibilities.

This realization also reshaped my understanding of what it means to educate. It isn't about adhering to a single model or system; it's about creating an environment where students can flourish in their own unique ways. The American education system may not rely on the strict rules and uniforms that many associate with traditional schooling, but its strength lies in its adaptability and its emphasis on fostering independence and creativity. It was a powerful reminder that sometimes, the paths we don't plan for turn out to be the most rewarding ones.

As I reflect on both my professional and personal journeys, I see how teaching and parenting have intertwined in ways I never expected. The lessons I've learned from my students about perseverance, growth, and the importance of seeing potential in every individual have enriched my life far beyond the classroom. And through my sons, I've come to appreciate the beauty of a system that encourages exploration and individuality, preparing students not just for exams but for life.

Interestingly, my journey of discovery didn't end there. That summer marked a turning point in my own story, as I made the decision to move to Egypt and continue teaching English, this time to high school students preparing for the Baccalauréat (Bac) exam. This move represented not only a shift in geography but also a new chapter of growth and adaptation as an educator.

In Egypt, I stepped into the structured world of the French learning system. It was a stark contrast to the flexibility and creativity of the American system, with its emphasis on rigor, precision, and discipline. Students were expected to adhere to a curriculum that left little room for deviation, yet the intensity of their studies inspired a deep sense of focus and commitment. As a teacher, I had to adapt my methods to fit this new environment while still holding onto the interactive, student-centered strategies I had cultivated in the United States.

Here, I became "Madame Nesreen," as is customary in French schools in Egypt, where teachers are addressed with a formal title. At first, it felt like stepping into an entirely different world, one where tradition and respect for hierarchy were woven deeply into the fabric of the educational system. But it also reminded me of a universal truth about teaching: no matter the system, the goal is the same, to inspire students to grow, to challenge them to think critically, and to prepare them for the future.

This experience opened my eyes to yet another way of teaching and learning, one that supported my understanding of education's many forms. It also reminded me of the adaptability required of teachers—how we must adjust to new systems, cultural expectations, and even different definitions of success. Standing at the front of that classroom in Cairo, I realized that education is not confined by borders or systems; it is a shared human endeavor, one that shapes minds and changes lives no matter where in the world it takes place.

Looking back, my time in Egypt felt like the natural continuation of my teaching journey, a step that connected my past experiences in Houston to a broader, more global perspective on education. It was a humbling reminder that while I was teaching, I was also learning about resilience, the universality of human potential, and the ways in which education transcends cultural boundaries.

Now, when I look back, I see that my journey was never just about teaching; it was about learning, growing, and becoming. It was about discovering that the impact we have on others often mirrors the impact they have on us. Every classroom, every student, and every challenge added a new layer to the person I've become. Teaching in America gave me the flexibility to innovate, while teaching in Egypt grounded me in the discipline of a structured system. Both experiences taught me that education, in all its forms, has the power to change lives, including my own.

As I turn this final page, I do so with a heart full of gratitude, knowing that every student, every challenge, and every moment of joy has been a part of the story that shaped me, both in America and beyond. My journey is one I will always carry with me, a testament to the transformative power of teaching and the endless possibilities of learning, a story that began in America, was deepened in Egypt, and continues to evolve here in the UK.

Teacher Tip

Take a moment now and then to pause and really reflect, not just on the lessons you've taught, but on how much you've grown along the way. Maybe you've become more flexible with different student needs, built stronger relationships, or tried out new teaching strategies that once felt out of reach. That progress matters. And so does noticing where you'd still like to grow.

You don't need a big routine, just small, honest moments of reflection. Jot down a few thoughts in a journal, look back at old lesson plans, or read through feedback from students or colleagues. Often, you'll spot quiet victories you didn't realize were there. And don't underestimate what your students can teach you—about resilience, curiosity, and even yourself. Your colleagues, too, can offer fresh ways of thinking that can shift your whole approach.

And please, celebrate your wins. Even the little ones. When a student finally gets something that's been tough for them, or when a colleague thanks you for your support, those are the moments that remind you why you teach. Reflection isn't just about looking back—it's about staying inspired for what's ahead, and becoming the kind of educator you're proud to be.

Parent Tip

It's easy to focus on grades and test scores, but your child's learning journey is about so much more than academics. It's also about growing as a person, building confidence, learning from mistakes, and bouncing back from tough days.

Celebrate the little wins, even the quiet ones. Talk through the challenges, and help them see that every step, no matter how small, is still progress. Most importantly, let them feel your steady support. Knowing that you believe in them, even when things get hard, is what helps them grow into strong, resilient individuals who are ready to take on the world.

23 Three Research-based Lesson Plans for Teachers

Throughout my teaching journey, I have come to realize that having the right resources at hand can make all the difference in creating engaging, effective lessons. This chapter consists of three lesson plans that I have developed and refined over the years. These plans incorporate a variety of teaching approaches, from nondirective methods to inquiry-based learning, and are designed to be adaptable to different classroom settings and student needs. The approach for the three lessons provided in this chapter came from a framework I studied in graduate school, but I've adapted it based on the real needs of my students. Every conversation will look different, but the heart of the lesson is the same: trust the child, believe in their voice, and walk with them as they find it.

***

Lesson Plan 1

Lesson Title: Your Ideas Are Valuable

Grade Level: Second Grade

Subject: Character Development

Approach: The Nondirective Model (building trust, guiding students toward self-discovery through supportive dialogue)

Big Idea

Every student has something valuable to share, but not every student feels safe enough to speak. This lesson helps children recognize their own voice, understand their fears, and take small, brave steps toward sharing their ideas with others.

Learning Objectives

By the end of this lesson, students will:

- Talk about a problem they're facing—academic or personal.
- Name their emotions and understand where they're coming from.
- Begin thinking about healthy, long-term ways to handle tough moments.

What You'll Need

Just a quiet, private moment, maybe during lunch, center time, or after a lesson. No handouts. No tech. Just space to connect.

Phase 1: Opening the Door, Defining the Helping Situation

This phase is all about setting the tone. You're not lecturing or "fixing"—you're noticing, caring, and gently inviting the student to share.

Example from the classroom:

Ryan is a bright second grader who shines in math—but he never shares in class. I decided to check in during a quiet lunch break.

Teacher (Mrs. Adams): "Ryan, I saw how you solved those tricky fraction problems today. That was some impressive thinking."

Ryan: "Thanks. I like fractions."

Mrs. Adams: "I think your classmates would've loved to hear how you figured it out. You explained it so clearly on paper."

Ryan (shrugs): "I don't think they'd care what I say."

Here, you gently open a door:

Mrs. Adams: "Why do you feel that way? Tell me more."

This question isn't about pushing, it's about saying, "I'm here. I care. Let's talk."

Phase 2: Digging Deeper—Exploring the Problem

Once trust is there, help the student name the challenge in their own words. This phase is about listening more than talking.

Ryan: "I don't want people to think I'm showing off. And what if I mess up? They might laugh."

Mrs. Adams: "So it sounds like you're worried about being judged, like people might think you're bragging, or they'll laugh if you make a mistake."

Ryan: "Yeah. That's why I keep quiet."

In this moment, you're showing the student they're not alone in those feelings, and that their emotions make sense.

Phase 3: Gentle Reflection—Developing Insight

Now, help the student look inward. This phase is about connecting dots between past and present.

Mrs. Adams: "Can you think of a time when you did feel good about sharing your ideas?"

Ryan (after a pause): "Last year, I used to raise my hand a lot. But then I heard some kids call me a 'know-it-all.' So I stopped."

Mrs. Adams: "That must've really hurt."

Ryan: "Yeah … I thought being quiet would be better. But it actually makes me feel worse."

Here, the student begins to recognize that avoiding the problem hasn't brought relief; it's just kept them from being themselves.

Phase 4: Making a Plan—Decision-making Together

This phase invites the student to think forward. You're not giving solutions; you're helping them come up with one.

Mrs. Adams: "What do you think could help you feel safer sharing in class again?"

Ryan: "Maybe … maybe you could talk to the class? Like remind them that it's okay to speak up?"

Mrs. Adams: "That's a great idea. How about we have a class talk about how everyone's voice matters—because it really does. Would you feel okay raising your hand again after that?"

Ryan (nods): "Yeah, I think so."

That "I think so" is gold. It means hope.

Phase 5: New Beginnings—Integration

This final step is where the growth becomes visible. You create a moment for the whole class to learn from this, without naming names or singling anyone out.

The Next Day:

During the morning meeting, Mrs. Adams leads a conversation on kindness and how important it is to encourage one another. The class discusses what it means to be a supportive listener.

Each student writes a short reflection:

"Why is it important to share your ideas, and how can we help each other feel safe doing it?"

That week, Ryan slowly begins to speak up again. The first time he answers, a few kids smile and nod. The second time, one says, "Good job, Ryan."

It's a small shift. But it's everything.

***

Lesson Plan 2

Lesson Title: Let's Discover Sentence Types—Together

Grade Level: Sixth Grade

Subject: ESL

Approach: Inductive Thinking—Let students notice, talk, and figure it out

Big Idea

We don't need to tell students the grammar rules right away. In this lesson, students discover them. Like little language detectives, they'll look at real sentences, spot punctuation clues, talk through patterns, and come to their own conclusions about how English sentences work.

They'll realize, on their own, that we use different sentence types to tell, ask, command, or exclaim. And that each one has its own punctuation mark.

Learning Outcomes

By the end of the lesson, your students will:

- Know the four sentence types (declarative, interrogative, imperative, exclamatory)
- Match each type with its end mark (period, question mark, exclamation point)
- Write their own examples and feel proud of doing so!

What You'll Need

- Prepared sentence strips (one example per strip)
- Colored markers
- Chart paper or poster paper
- Sticky tack or tape
- Whiteboard and markers
- Optional: Visual sentence starters or scaffold cards for ELs

Phase 1: Warm-Up—Looking for Clues

Break students into small groups (3–4 per group). Hand each group a handful of sentence strips, some statements, some questions, some commands, some exciting blurts.

Let them read quietly first. Then, ask them to talk together:

- What do you notice about these sentences?
- How do they sound?
- What punctuation do they end with?

Let them explore without labels, just look, read, and discuss.

Examples:

- I like donuts.
- Can you help me?
- Close the door.
- That's amazing!

Phase 2: Talking It Out ... What Do You See?

Now guide them gently. Ask:

- "What kind of sentence is this?"
- "Is it telling, asking, commanding, or showing feeling?"

Have students jot down ideas. It's okay if they don't know the grammar names yet, this is about noticing, not memorizing.

Phase 3: Sort and Group

Let the groups now sort their sentence strips into categories they create. Don't give away the answers. They'll start building logic like:

- "These all tell us something."
- "These are all questions."
- "These sound like warnings or excitement."

You can walk around and listen for reasoning. Ask gentle questions:

- "Why do these go together?"
- "What makes these feel similar?" (This is where real thinking happens.)

Phase 4: Name What You've Found

Now's the time to help students label the sentence types:

- Declarative for statements
- Interrogative for questions
- Imperative for commands
- Exclamatory for strong emotions

Each group creates a mini poster or chart to show their categories. One student becomes the Scribe, another the Presenter. Let them share their "discovery" with the class.

You'll feel the pride in their voices **because** they figured it out themselves.

Phase 5: Whole-class Wrap-up and Creation

On the board, draw four big columns: one for each sentence type. Invite students to place their sentence strips in the right spot, collaboratively.

Then, ask everyone to come up with one of each sentence type:

- A sentence that tells
- A sentence that asks
- A sentence that commands
- A sentence that shouts with feeling

They can write them down or say them out loud. Post them up to celebrate their learning!

Support for English Learners

- Pair ELs with encouraging peers, they'll learn through conversation
- Offer sentence frames like: Can I …, Please …, Wow …, I think …
- Use visuals, gestures, or translation apps to clarify tricky words
- Celebrate ideas first, grammar perfection can come later

Why Students Love This Lesson

This lesson makes grammar feel like a puzzle, not a lecture. It lets students see how English works, not just hear about it. And it's especially powerful for ELs, who benefit from talking, moving, noticing, and creating together.

***

Lesson Plan 3

Lesson Title: Exploring the Food Groups: A Hands-on Inquiry Experience

Grade Level: 3–6

Language Level: ESL Beginners to Intermediate

Subject: ESL (Science & Language Integration)

Instructional Approach: Inquiry Method—Let students lead the learning with curiosity and conversation

Lesson Purpose

Instead of starting with a chart or a lecture, this lesson begins with a question, and a table full of food.

Students are invited to observe, touch, smell, and wonder. They'll explore real food samples, talk about what makes them different, and then begin organizing them based on shared traits. Along the way, they'll learn the names of the six food groups and the descriptive language that goes with them, all while having fun and learning from each other.

This isn't just a vocabulary lesson. It's an experience that helps students connect language, health, and real-world thinking.

Student-friendly Objectives

By the end of the lesson, students will:

- Notice and describe what makes different foods unique
- Group foods based on their shared traits (e.g., texture, color, taste, nutritional purpose)
- Name each of the six food groups in English
- Create new examples from their own lives and cultures to add to each category.

What You'll Need:

- Small food samples (real, plastic, or photo cutouts) from each group:
- Grains, vegetables, fruits, oils, meat & beans, and milk/dairy
- Chart paper
- Markers
- Space for group work and movement
- Optional: Printed food group visuals or word banks for language support

Phase 1: Let Them Wonder (Sparking Curiosity)

As students walk into the room, they'll find a colorful display of food samples placed in random order, no labels, just real objects. Bananas next to bread. Cheese beside beans. Olive oil, apples, rice, and yogurt, all mixed up.

Invite students to explore using all their senses (except taste, for safety):

- "Look closely."
- "Touch if it's safe."
- "Smell gently."
- "What do you notice?"

Let them talk freely with a partner or group. Then ask:

"What do you see that makes some foods different from others?"

Let students share their ideas:

- "This one is sweet."
- "That one is soft."
- "This looks like it gives energy."

Then say:

"Today, you're the investigators. Your job is to figure out what makes these foods different, and how we might group them."

Phase 2: Team Investigators (Structuring the Problem)

Split students into small groups. Give each group chart paper and markers. Their task: explore the food table again and start taking notes.

Encourage them to:

- Touch or point to foods
- Use language like "This is like … " or "This feels … "
- Draw pictures if they can't write the word yet
- Support them with vocabulary visuals or word banks as needed.

Phase 3: Making a Discovery (Identifying the Groups)

As students organize their ideas, gently guide them toward discovering that these foods naturally fit into six major groups:

- Grains
- Fruits
- Vegetables
- Oils
- Milk/Dairy
- Meat & Beans (or Protein)

Rather than giving this information immediately, elicit answers by asking prompting questions:

- "Are there foods that grow in trees?"
- "Which ones give us energy?"
- "What do we drink with cereal?"
- Once students begin to spot the patterns, help them label each category and write the group names on their charts.

Phase 4: Explaining Their Thinking (Presenting the Findings)

Now the groups get to shine.

Each team presents:

- Their food group names
- What traits helped them sort the foods
- New examples they can add (from their culture, lunchbox, or imagination)

For example:

- "Apples are fruit. They are sweet."
- "Beans are protein. They help muscles."
- "Bread is a grain. It gives energy."

Encourage visuals and student-led pointing or drawing during presentations. For ELs, body language and visuals can be just as powerful as words.

Differentiation Ideas

For Grades 3–4 (Beginners):

- Use sentence frames like:
- "Milk is dairy." "Rice is grains."
- Provide picture dictionaries or bilingual labels.
- Focus on key nouns and adjectives: sweet, soft, yellow, hot, cold

For Grades 5–6 (Intermediate):

- Encourage full sentences and reasoning:
  - "Avocados belong to the oil group because they have healthy fats."
  - "Yogurt is part of the dairy group because it is made from milk."
  - Introduce more advanced vocabulary: energy, vitamins, nutrients

Why This Lesson Works

This lesson honors how children learn best, through their senses, their voices, and their curiosity. That is why bringing *Realia*, real tangible objects to the class is crucial for learning.

It creates space for:

- Language learning rooted in real-world experience
- Peer conversations that build confidence
- Valuing cultural knowledge (what students eat at home)
- A hands-on, fun experience that sticks in memory

Students won't just remember the food groups. They'll remember the moment they discovered them for themselves.

Teacher Tip

Some of the best teaching tools come from unexpected places, whether it's a new website you stumble upon, a strategy shared in an online teacher group, or a tip picked up at a conference. Stay curious, stay connected, and keep exploring what's out there. The more you grow, the more your students will, too.

Parent Tip

As a parent, you have a powerful role to play in your child's learning journey. One of the most meaningful things you can do is simply sit beside your child and explore new things together. Whether it's reading a story, playing a language game, or watching an educational video, these shared moments do more than reinforce learning, they show your child that you care, that you're proud, and that you're walking this path with them. So take a little time, even if it's just ten minutes a day, to discover these resources side by side. It's not just about learning, it's about connection.